Water and Storm Polemics Against Baalism in the Deuteronomic History

American University Studies

Series VII
Theology and Religion
Vol. 150

PETER LANG
New York • San Francisco • Bern • Baltimore
Frankfurt am Main • Berlin • Wien • Paris

Fred E. Woods

Water and Storm Polemics Against Baalism in the Deuteronomic History

PETER LANG
New York • San Francisco • Bern • Baltimore
Frankfurt am Main • Berlin • Wien • Paris

Library of Congress Cataloging-in-Publication Data

Woods, Fred E.
  Water and storm polemics against Baalism in the Deuteronomic
history / Fred E. Woods.
    p. cm. — (American university studies. Series VII, Theology and
religion ; vol. 150)
  Includes bibliographical references and index.
  1. D document (Biblical criticism).   2. Baal (Deity)—Cult—Biblical
teaching.   3. Bible. O.T. Deuteronomy—Criticism, interpretation, etc.
4. Bible. O.T. Former Prophets—Criticism, interpretation, etc.
5. Water in the Bible.   6. Storms in the Bible.   I. Title.   II. Series.
BS1181.17.W66   1994   222'.06—dc20   93-2973
  ISBN 0-8204-2111-1   CIP
  ISSN 0740-0446

Die Deutsche Bibliothek-CIP-Einheitsaufnahme

Woods, Fred:
Water and storm polemics against Baalism in the Deuteronomic
history / Fred E. Woods.—New York; Berlin; Bern; Frankfurt/M.;
Paris; Wien: Lang, 1994
  (American university studies : Ser. VII, Theology and religion ;
Vol. 150)
    ISBN 0-8204-2111-1
NE: American university studies/24

The paper in this book meets the guidelines for permanence and
durability of the Committee on Production Guidelines for
Book Longevity of the Council on Library Resources.

© Peter Lang Publishing, Inc., New York 1994

To JoAnna,
whose price is far above rubies.

ACKNOWLEDGMENTS

I wish to express my appreciation to my doctoral committee at the University of Utah, namely Dr. Harris Lenowitz (chairman), Dr. Lawrence C. Loeb, and Dr. Philip C. Hammond for their guidance in the research underlying this work. To my Hebrew tutor, Michal Nevo, I extend my deep appreciation for her willingness to share of herself and her people and teach me more than just the Hebrew language.

Also of invaluable editing assistance were Marilyn Rish Parks, the office of Don Norton, and several able colleagues at Brigham Young University who reviewed the manuscript. The Brigham Young University Religious Studies Center and the Foundation for Ancient Research and Mormon Studies (F.A.R.M.S.) contributed funds for the publication of this work, and I gratefully acknowledge their support. John H. Heath typeset the manuscript and, along with Michael J. Flamini, Kathy Iwasaki, and the staff of Peter Lang, Inc., provided valuable support and guidance throughout the publication process.

I extend my gratitude to my parents, sister, children, and extended family for their continual love and support. Most especially I thank my wife JoAnna, my dearest friend and companion for her undying confidence in me. Finally, I acknowledge with much gratitude the hand of God in this undertaking and in all areas of my life. To all of you, thank you.

CONTENTS

INTRODUCTION

M an's physiological needs are his most fundamental concerns. Among these needs, water is of paramount importance. The agrarian peoples of the ancient Middle East were acutely aware of the most basic equation: water = life. The relatively arid climate with its seasonal rainfalls magnified the need for this sustaining element into a daily concern. In man's attempt to explain the uncertainty of his existence and thereby to gain some control over it, he developed gods to serve as intercessory, intermediary, figures between him and nature. The importance of nature gods in religious beliefs and attitudes was shaped significantly by man's dependence upon water and his attempt to influence its supply.

The diverse religious attitudes of the ancient Egyptians and Sumerians illustrate the relationship between geographic and climatic conditions and theology. The Sumerians lived among two great rivers, the Tigris and the Euphrates. The water supply was highly unpredictable, with storms, floods and droughts creating a fragile environment.

These conditions may have contributed to a pessimistic quality in Sumerian religion. The gods could not be fully trusted, were themselves not free of fate, and afterlife was viewed as uncertain.[1] H. and H. A. Frankfort suggest the ancient people reasoned that "If the rivers refused to rise, it is not suggested that the lack of rainfall on distant mountains adequately explains the calamity...the river, or the gods, must be angry with the people."[2]

On the other hand, the Egyptian religions tended to be optimistic, perhaps because of a steady water supply. Egyptian records calculate that the Nile would flood consistently at the same time each season.[3] This created an environment of stability unknown in Mesopotamia. This natural regularity may have influenced the Egyptians and bolstered a religion filled with optimism and trust in divine powers and the afterlife.[4]

When the Hebrew tribes left the stable environment of Egypt and headed toward the land of Canaan, they encountered a people who worshipped the storm god called Baal and his retinue. Such an encounter created a culture conflict. Israel had been led by Yahweh through the sea and the desert, but as she entered the new land, Israel asked, "Was Yahweh also the god of Canaan?"

As the Israelites settled in Canaan, they were tempted to ask their Canaanite neighbors, "How does your garden grow?" Such inquiry was seen by later writers as having led to eventual apostasy and exile as Israel became idolatrous and eventually drowned in Baalism. The salient historical events that led to her entrance into the land of Canaan and her subsequent exit to Babylon are interpreted in the strata of the Hebrew Bible known as the Deuteronomic History (Deuteronomy-Kings). It is within this corpus of literature that there is the frequency of polemical language against Baalism (the storm god Baal and his retinue). The present study explores the symbolic function of language in the Deuteronomic History which deals with water and storm as polemics against Baalism.

The first major modern work on water in the Hebrew Bible was Raphael Patai's *Ha Mayim* (1936), a general treatise (written in Hebrew), on how the language of water operates in the Bible. In 1958, Philippe Reymond wrote *L'eau, sa vie, et sa signification dans l'Ancien Testament*. Reymond gives a general overview of how water terms are used in the Hebrew Bible.

In 1985 John Day produced *God's Conflict with the Dragon and the Sea: Echoes of a Canaanite Myth in the Old Testament*, which is a general treatise discussing God's power over water and its sea monsters. Carola Kloos wrote *Yhwh's Combat with the Sea: A Canaanite Tradition in the Religion of Ancient Israel* in 1986, and it also deals with God's struggle to control the waters.

Most recently, (1987), William Propp published *Water in the Wilderness. A Biblical Motif and its Mythological Background*, which investigates the specific relationship between Israelite historiographical traditions and Israel's mythic patterns borrowed from earlier Canaanite culture. Propp's focus is on the cosmogonic pattern of the restriction of the Red Sea, followed by the irrigation of the dry land. This theme is then traced through the Bible. These works have opened the way to address the issue of water and storm polemics in the Deuteronomic History arising within the conflict between Baalism and Yahwism.

In 1964 Norman C. Habel published *Yahweh versus Baal: A Conflict of Religious Cultures*, his study of the conflict between Baal and Yahweh. Habel's study was a broad overview of examples of conflict extending to the perimeters of the text of the entire Hebrew Bible. Although Habel touched on the explicit prophetic reaction to Baal worship, he did not explore the implicit polemics that used various aspects of water and storm as a polemic against Baal worship. In this same year Frank E. Eakin, Jr., completed his dissertation entitled, "The Relationship of Yahwism and Baalism During the Pre-Exilic Period." Eakin's thesis was a historical study which advocated that there was no overt conflict between Yahweh and Baal until Elijah combated the prophets of Baal on Mount Carmel.

The work which most closely resembles my study is *The Stories of Elijah and Elisha as Polemics Against Baal Worship*, (1968), by Leah Bronner, a revised and shortened version of Bronner's thesis. Dr. Bronner regards all the stories of Elijah and Elisha as deliberate polemics against Baal worship. I agree that the water/storm stories are indeed polemics against Baalism, but feel Bronner's comparative study of Ugaritic texts and Israelite literature has gone beyond the evidence by suggesting that all of the stories of Elijah and Elisha are polemics against Baalism. P.A.H. De Boer concurs and asserts in a review of Bronner's work that as a comparative study of religions, it is all in all a failure.[5] Furthermore, De Boer points out that "Dr. Bronner's bibliography is very incomplete and inaccurate."[6] This is evidenced by the fact that *none* of the works mentioned above is listed in Bronner's bibliography. (Bronner should here be credited with the fact that Propp's work was written several years after the publication of her book; therefore, it is obvious that she did not have access to Propp's study.)

There is a need to address the specific issue of water/storm literature in the Deuteronomic History of which the Elijah and Elisha stories form a portion. Within this stratum of text, there is strong evidence of explicit polemics against Baalism. However, the evidence of implicit polemics, relying upon various aspects of water and storm language, has been largely overlooked—a matter corrected by this dissertation. The methodology that will be used herein to explore the issue of water/storm polemics in the Deuteronomic History is derived from elements of the historical critical approach as well as the text critical approach. In addition to these approaches, the Ras Shamra Texts will serve as a control mechanism. The method of transliteration used in this work follows the *Encyclopedia Judaica* style.

Chapter 1 begins with an overview of the Ras Shamra texts and the Ugaritic pantheon with an emphasis on the most active deity at Ugarit, Baal Hadad the storm god. Chapter 2 surveys the framework of the Deuteronomic History. This is followed by a discussion of the severe polemics against syncretism within this framework. The specific role of Deuteronomy within the Deuteronomic History is then addressed in relation to its authorship, date, structure, style, and content. Finally, the polemics against Baalism are viewed within the covenantal context of the Book of Deuteronomy.

Chapter 3 focuses on the textual evidence of the polemical language of water and storm in the Book of Joshua and the Book of Judges. Chapter 4 examines the textual evidence from the Books of Samuel, and Chapter 5 treats the textual evidence in the Books of Kings. Finally, a conclusion summarizes and analyzes the evidence.

It is the thesis of this dissertation that the abundant usage of water and storm language in the Deuteronomic History is aimed at a literary attack against Baalism. The literature conveys the purpose of the Deuteronomic writers which is to declare a monotheistic message of Yahweh's omnipotent power, as well as his divine ability to provide and protect his covenant people.

NOTES

1. Milton Covensky, *The Ancient Near East Tradition* (New York: Harper & Row, 1966), x, 15.

2. H. Frankfort and H. A. Frankfort, *The Intellectual Adventure of Ancient Man* (Chicago: University of Chicago Press, 1946), 15.

3. Ibid. Although the records confirm that the Nile flooded at the same time annually, the pharaoh consistently offered gifts to the Nile when it was approaching its appointed time to rise.

4. Covensky, *The Ancient Near East Tradition*, xi.

5. P. A. H. De Boer, review of *The Stories of Elijah and Elisha as Polemics Against Baal Worship*, by Leah Bronner, in *Vetus Testamentum* 19 (1969): 269.

6. Ibid.

CHAPTER 1

BAALISM

Scholars generally agree that to acquire an understanding of Baalism, i.e., Canaanite religion per se, the principal literary sources are the Ugaritic Texts.[1] Ugarit itself was not discovered until 1928, when a peasant stumbled upon a tombstone just north of Minet el-Beida on the north Syrian coast. The French authorities of antiquities were then contacted, and Claude F. A. Schaeffer began excavations in April 1929 in the area of Minet el-Beida. A short time later, Schaeffer moved his excavations a little to the east to the tell of Ras Shamra, which proved to be the ancient site of Ugarit. Schaeffer's excavations revealed five major levels.[2] Level one, dating from about 1500–1200 B.C., contained the most valuable materials, including the Ugaritic texts. The texts were written in an alphabetic cuneiform language that was yet undeciphered. By June 1930 these tablets were deciphered and the Ugaritic language discovered.[3]

The tablets shed abundant light on the Canaanite pantheon of which Baal-Hadad was the god par excellence. Before the Ugaritic texts were excavated, the Baalism which the Hebrew prophets adamantly battled was little understood. With this discovery, the Baal texts could now speak for themselves. Paul L. Watson equates this discovery with a comparative reading of the Essenes in Josephus with the Qumran literature we now possess.[4]

The use of this evidence as the major source of Canaanite religion, however, does have its limitations in relation to this study. The first is whether the city of Ugarit represents a typical Canaanite society. Cautions William Jobling, "To designate Ugarit as typically Canaanite and, therefore, Ugaritic material and literary materials as being typical of the people of Canaan...is to proceed further than the extant evidence permits."[5] Furthermore, Jobling points out that "Ugarit was a great center of culture amalgamation and diffusion and in this sense may not have been a good example of any one particular aspect of the culture of Syria or Palestine."[6] The second is the chronological concern that the Ugaritic literature, dated from the 15th–13th centuries B.C., occurs several centuries earlier than the final editing of the Deuteronomic History around the time of the exile. Third, there is the issue of different geographic locations, the ancient city of Ugarit is located quite a distance to the north of the land of Canaan.

In spite of these apparent limitations, William F. Albright argues that Ugarit plays a vital role in understanding Canaanite culture and religion. Though it is unclear to what degree Ugarit was a part of the land of Canaan, because of the fluctuation of Canaan's northern border over the centuries, Albright still maintains that the language and culture of Ugarit is in harmony with that of Canaan. Consequently, he refers to the Ugaritic material as North Canaanite. Furthermore, he points quite convincingly to the ample evidence that the Ugaritic deities were worshipped not only at Ugarit, but also in Syria, Canaan, and even Egypt.[7]

I concur with Frank Eakin, who maintains that while we should recognize the apparent dangers of equating Canaan with Ugarit, "nonetheless a cultural homogeneity existed along the Levant during the cultural zenith of Ugarit. To describe the character of Ugaritic worship, therefore, is to portray also the nature of Canaanite worship."[8]

MAJOR CANAANITE DEITIES

The major gods of the Canaanite pantheon are El, Baal, Dagan, Yam, and Mot; the goddesses of primary import are Athirat, Anat, and Ashtarte. It is a very difficult task to understand the nature and relationship between these and other Canaanite deities because of their fluidity. Mitchell Dahood explains that "the character and functions of the gods are subject to such fluctuations that to determine their nature and qualities, or to fix their relations with one another is often impossible."[9] However, Baalism was a fertility cult, which functioned to bring fertility to the earth. This cultic activity was widespread in the community. Of this, Eakin writes:

> The sensuality was not restricted to priests and priestesses; rather, all devotees of Baal encouraged his union with Anat by sexual union themselves, males identifying with Baal and females with Anat. The artifacts relating to both male and female deities point

to their sensual orientation, but most especially is this true of the goddesses.[10]

Archaeological evidence has revealed a common Canaanite religious culture extending from Ugarit to southern Palestine. Baal figurines have been excavated throughout this area. The figurines excavated from such sites as Lachish and Megiddo correspond quite closely to Baal figurines from Ugarit, dated to the same era of the Late Bronze period.[11] A large number of female figurines have also been excavated from Palestine. James Pritchard, who has done extensive research in this area, concludes: "The one feature common to all the figurines and plaques studied here is that of nudity and in most of the cases an emphasis upon the reproductive feature of the female figure."[12] This evidence suggests that the Canaanite religion was closely associated with fertility, which led to a "Kulturkampf" as the Hebrew tribes entered Canaan and were exposed to these fertility cults.[13]

Athirat

In the Ugaritic pantheon, Athirat is recognized as the supreme fertility goddess. She is the wife of the chief god, El, and the suckling mother to their seventy sons, who are also gods. The epithet by which she is best known is *rbt a trt ym* (Lady Asherah of the Sea). Her servant is called "the fisherman of Lady Asherah of the Sea." Kaiser asserts that her epithet is a nominal form of the verb *ʾtr* meaning "to walk, go straight, to tread."[14] This combined evidence suggests that perhaps Athirat was connected with the idea of a goddess of provision who not only created life, but also sustained it through her apparent power to tread the sea and her ability to provide food from the sea. Perhaps she was associated with fishing. In any case, the text gives no further clues to the meaning of the epithet.[15]

Athirat is known in the Hebrew Bible by the name Asherah, which occurs in the Hebrew Bible forty times.[16] Although she is known at Ugarit as El's wife, the Hebrew Bible designates Asherah as the consort of Baal (Judg. 3:7).[17] This appears to be linked to the notion that as Baal gradually displaced El as the chief Canaanite deity, Asherah became associated with Baal rather than El. Ulf Oldenburg argues convincingly that "the evidence from the Hebrew Bible shows that already by the times of the Hebrew judges Asherah was regarded as the consort of *Baʿal*, whom he had taken from the Canaanite El when he usurped his throne."[18]

In the Hebrew Bible, the Hebrew word *asherah* has more than one meaning. It can be taken either as the proper name of a Canaanite goddess or as a cultic object.[19] For example, 1 Kings 4:19 speaks of "the four hundred prophets of Asherah who eat at Jezebel's table." In 1 Kings 15:13 there is evidence of an image made for Asherah. On the other hand, *asherah* could also mean a sacred tree or pole which was built near an altar and which stood as a symbol of the goddess Asherah (1 Kgs. 16:33; 2 Kgs. 13:6; 17:6; 18:4; 21:3; 23:6, 15).[20] John Day writes of the relationship of the cultic object to Asherah: "That the Asherah cult object symbolized the goddess Asherah seems clear enough, but this does not necessarily require it to have been an actual image."[21]

Deuteronomy portrays Yahweh speaking adamantly against the cultic worship of the asherah: "You shall not set up a sacred pole beside the altar of the Lord your God, or erect a stone pillar; for such Yahweh your God detests" (Deut. 16:21). Such sacred poles were to be destroyed by fire (Deut. 12:3).[22]

Anat

Another goddess who figures prominently in the Ugaritic pantheon is Anat, portrayed in the Ugaritic texts as Baal's sister and consort. Her epithet is "the virgin Anath."[23] She, like Athirat, was a goddess of fertility. However, Anat also appears in the Ugaritic texts as a violent goddess of love and war who fights for Baal. In *The Violent Goddess Anat in the Ras Shamra Texts*, Arvid S. Kapelrud states that "she was a goddess who ravaged in blood, who was the sign and symbol of battle, fighting, blood and death."[24]

Anat was worshipped throughout the ancient world from Egypt to Mesopotamia.[25] The Ugaritic texts provide the most complete information on her distinct characteristics. Albright suggested that the meaning of the name Anat "probably meant originally 'sign, indication of purpose, active will' and was originally applied to the personified or hypostatized will of Baal."[26] However, Dr. Ariella Goldberg has more recently demonstrated that Anat may be related to the Hebrew root $^c n h$, meaning "to have sexual intercourse."[27] This is more probable when we consider the fact that Anat is depicted as a female calf that erotically mates with Baal,[28] and that the Canaanite cult at Ugarit is pregnant with the notion of fertility rites.

Anat is represented in the Hebrew Bible by the place names Beth-Anat[29] and Anatot.[30] The personal name of Shamgar ben Anat (Judg. 3:31; 5:6), as well as these place names, provide evidence that Anat was in fact worshipped in Israel. However, no further information is available in the Hebrew Bible concerning her. Kapelrud provides the following explanation:

> Possibly more information about her might have been found, if she had not been so completely confused with other goddesses by traditionists and authors. The Israelite and Judean traditionists were not always able to keep the different goddesses apart.... Since they did not even want to pronounce the names of these despised goddesses, the confusion was soon complete.[31]

Ashtarte

The third major Canaanite goddess at Ugarit was Ashtarte. Although she does not figure as prominently in the Ugaritic mythical texts as Athirat or Anat, Ashtarte occupies a secure place in the Ugaritic pantheon, as evidenced by the offering lists of the religious texts.[32] She, like Anat, is depicted as a goddess of fertility, love, and war. We can surmise that she is associated with Baal from her epithet, "name of Baal."[33]

In the Hebrew Bible the equivalent of Ashtarte is Ashtoret. This appears to be a dysphemism created by a Hebrew scribe who "retained the consonants and substituted the vowels of *b-s-th* (boshet), 'shame' in the last two syllables."[34] This name is attested in singular form only in 1 Kings 11:5, 33 and 2 Kings 23:13. The plural form of Astarot is more common and is used in relation to Canaanite fertility worship in general to represent the manifestation of this goddess.[35]

"The three goddesses, Astarte (Ashtaroth) Anath, and Asherah, present the most complex pattern of relations,"[36] Albright notes of these major goddesses. This is especially true in the Hebrew Bible because of the ambiguity of the terminology surrounding each of these goddesses. However, the Ras Shamra texts aid in retaining their separate identity.[37] Although each of the goddesses maintains a distinction of her own, the characteristic of each can be merged into a single theme, cultic fertility rites.

El

In 1955 Marvin H. Pope published *El in the Ugaritic Texts*, the most comprehensive treatise on the god El. According to Pope, "the word il(u), West Semitic *el*, is common to all the Semitic languages except Ethiopic, as the general appellative meaning 'god' in the broadest sense."[38] However, he later notes it is also used to designate the proper name of a specific deity.[39]

The god El, patriarch of the Ugaritic pantheon, fathered seventy sons with the aid of his wife Athirat (Asherah). A bronze statuette of El was found in the twenty-third campaign at Ugarit. El was dressed in a full robe, wore a crown with two horns protruding from it, and had the face of a kind old man.[40] The epithets of El describe him as a "Creator of creatures," "the father of mankind," "god of mercy," "king," and "the bull El."[41] Such titles characterize a god who is benevolent yet powerful. Scholars have maintained, however, that such an image is merely titular in the Ugaritic myths. According to Pope, "that El has a position of high honor in the Ugaritic pantheon seems inconvertible. Yet as has been already noted, there are indications that his exalted position is more or less titulary."[42] Albright concurs with Pope: "In the epics El is certainly no more than the titular head of the pantheon and part of the time he seems quite otiose."[43] Dahood adds that in the Ugaritic material, "El appears as a remote and shadowy figure who lives at a great distance, 'a thousand plains, ten thousand fields' from Canaan, 'at the sources of the two rivers, in the midst of the fountains of the two deeps.'"[44]

By the time the Ugaritic texts reached their present form, the Canaanites certainly viewed El as a less prominent deity than Baal.[45] Perhaps one of the reasons for this was that El's abode may have been viewed as out of sight and thus out of mind. Unlike Baal and Dagan, he did not have a temple at Ugarit, where cultic sacrifice took place.[46] Yet, before this time, El appears to have been the true supreme head. John Gray explains,

> it is to the more primitive stratum of religion that El, with his social interest, belongs. In spite of later developments, however, the Semites of Ugarit were so far true to their primitive tradition that in the 14th century they still regarded El as the senior deity, though his position, broadly speaking, is rather an honorary one, at least in the fertility-cult, where the most active deity is Baal.[47]

Pope argues that Baal displaced El in the fourteenth century B. C. E. because of a general cultural change which took place, and that although El retained his prestige and title of former days, his authority as the supreme deity was gone.[48] A quarter-century later, Conrad E. L'Heurex vehemently disagreed with Pope's position that Baal displaced El.[49]

His argument was that El retained his ultimate authority throughout the Ugaritic myths. Pope addressed the issue of the status of El at Ugarit in a paper written thirty-two years after his book. In it he responded to L'Heurex:

> L'Heurex's view that El "is alive and well, presiding over gods and men as the ultimate source of authority in the cosmos" is more a confession of faith than a critical diagnosis of the problems provoked by the Ugaritic mythological texts. In polytheism there are always reasons for the king to worry about being overthrown when the divine realm is patterned after the human where even kings grow old and are some-times overthrown or otherwise eased out of power before they die. There are at least hints in the Ugaritic myths that El...was forced to give way to the younger stronger god of the storm.[50]

Baal-Hadad

The most active deity both at Ras Shamra and in the Canaanite pantheon of the Hebrew Bible is Baal, the god of the storm.[51] He is most often referred to by the common semitic noun *b^{c}l* meaning "owner, master, husband or lord."[52] This noun could be used as a title for a man or a god, and at Ugarit, Baal is used about forty times as a generic term.[53] However, this term developed into the proper name of a specific god also called Hadad, who is designated by the term Baal about 160 times in the Ugaritic texts, while Baal as a proper name is attested with the epithet *aliyn* meaning "mighty" sixty-five times.[54] This title *aliyn b^{c}l*, meaning "Most Mighty Baal," provides strong evidence that Baal is in fact the proper name of a god.

The name Hadad itself occurs only seventeen times in the Ugaritic texts[55]—an interesting fact in that it seems to relate to the notion of calling a specific deity "lord" to avoid repeating the sacred name of a deity.[56] This would be particularly true with Hadad, the supreme god at Ugarit.

The name Hadad is also attested in Akkadian where it may be translated as "thunderer."[57] This is most appropriate because Baal is associated with storm and is portrayed with "his weapon, the lightning, and his voice, the thunder."[58] Kapelrud provides a detailed description of Baal-Hadad from a stele excavated at Ras Shamra. He states:

In his uplifted right hand, Baal holds a thunderbolt, and in his left hand a representation of lightning in the form of a spear. The horns on the helmet recall the bull, the symbol of fertility. The club and spear indicate that this is a deity of rain and thunder, who, by sending the rain, ensures growth and increase in the fields and pastures.[59]

The mythic texts reveal that the abode of Baal-Hadad is at Mount Saphon, where he reigns, as one of his epithets indicates, as Lord of the earth. From his home he rules over all aspects of water and storm, including lightning, thunder, rain, dew, and clouds. In fact, one of his epithets refers to him as the "rider of the clouds," and another, "the good exalted one...who manifests his goodness and sovereignty by sending rain and fertility to the earth."[60] Of Baal sending the appropriate quantity of water to fructify the earth, J. C. De Moor observes:

In these semiarid regions, all life was dependent on a sufficient amount of precipitation. Therefore, Baal is the "Almighty,"...the "Exalted One,"...the "Sovereign Lord of the Earth,"...the king above whom no other can stand, the one who gives substance to all living creatures. When his sweet rain revives the field and seed, the heads of the peasant farmers are lifted up.... But when he withdraws and the parched land cannot be plowed or the vegetation withers, this naturally gives rise to despair. It is no wonder that a myth was created to attempt to explain the change in the seasons.[61]

In the Hebrew Bible, Baal is referred to more than any other Canaanite deity. The divine name of Baal occurs seventy-six times in the Hebrew Bible—eighteen times in the plural and fifty-eight times in the singular, the latter always accompanied by the definite article.[62] M. J. Mulder states that "the OT does not reveal whether another unknown divine name lies hidden behind the name Baal, e.g., Hadad. However, it does confirm the impression made by the Ugaritic texts that it has in mind Baal par excellence, the god of storm and fertility, who appears in different local manifestations and nuances."[63] Oldenburg reveals his opinion not only as to the identity of the name Baal in the Hebrew text, but also concerning the feelings of a faithful Yahwist for this god, is that the storm god Baal Hadad is portrayed as more wicked, immoral, and abominable than any other god.[64]

This strong denunciation of Baal lends itself to the notion that the Baalistic cult had deeply penetrated the Israelite soil. Otherwise, the issue would not have unleashed such a vehement literary attack against Baalism.

Dagan

As mentioned, El fathered seventy gods in the Ugaritic pantheon. However, Baal is called *bn dgn* (the son of dagan) eleven times in the Ugaritic mythological texts.[65] Although Baal is also called the son of El, this seems to reflect a change which had taken place when new gods such as Dagan and Baal entered the Ugaritic pantheon.[66]

Dahood suggests that the cult of Dagan had its roots in Upper Mesopotamia about the time of Sargon I (2360 B.C.) and that he was added by the Canaanites to the Ugaritic pantheon following the typical pattern of religious syncretism.[67] Oldenburg maintains that the Amorites worshipped Dagan and Baal-Hadad at such places as Mari and later brought these gods to the Canaanite pantheon at Ugarit.[68] He further argues that the primordial home of Dagan was at Tutal, in the Middle Euphrates region. This is supported by the fact that even in the Ugaritic texts Dagan's home, *ttlh* (Tutul), occurs.[69] Although evidence confirms that Dagan and Baal-Hadad were worshipped together in Mesopotamia before Ugarit, it seems that as Baal-Hadad entered the Ugaritic pantheon, he was naturally adopted into the family of El, although his family tie with Dagan was in no way severed.[70]

The word *dgn* means "grain" in Ugaritic, Hebrew, and Phoenician.[71] In Ugaritic the name is *dagan*. However, because of the Canaanite shift, in Hebrew the name is vocalized *dagon*. Throughout Mesopotamia, Dagan is thus viewed as a grain-fertility god. However, in all the places Dagan was worshipped, no mythological texts provide information on his character.[72] This is also true at Ugarit, where Dagan is mentioned in the mythic texts only as the father of Baal-Hadad.

Although Dagan does not play a major role in these texts, he does occupy a distinct position at Ugarit, as evidenced by sacrificial lists and a temple dedicated to him.[73] Schaeffer notes that Dagan's temple had the same plan and dimensions as that of his popular son Baal.[74] On the basis of this evidence, his influence in the cultic life of the people at Ugarit cannot be dismissed, nor his influence in the Hebrew Bible under the name of Dagon.[75]

Yam

Yam is the firstborn son of Asherah and El and the first enemy that Baal encounters. Yam appears twice in the sacrificial lists. His epithets are *zbl* (prince) and *mdd il* (beloved of El). His complete name is (*zbl ym ṯpṭ nhr*), which means "Prince Sea, Judge River."[76] Yam is the god of the sea, but as Theodore Gaster explains, "of the sea in an extended sense, which includes all lakes, rivers and other inland expanses of water, such as were considered in ancient thought to be fed by the upsurging of the subterranean ocean."[77]

By the time the Ugaritic mythological texts were written, the battle against the sea and the sea monster were one in the same. Yam was fused with *Ltn* (Lotan), the sea serpent,[78] a name related to Leviathan, which is one of the names of the sea dragon whom Yahweh conquers in the Hebrew Bible.[79] In the Ugaritic mythological texts, prince Baal is victorious in his battle against prince Yam, the lord of the sea. This defeat guaranteed that Yam would be contained and that there would be dry land, and it also posed the question of who would rule the dry land. The answer came when a temple was constructed for Baal, who reigned from his palace as lord of the earth.[80]

Mot

Mot, whose name means "death," is also a son of Asherah and El and is the chief enemy of Baal. He is the god of aridity, sterility, and death whose habitation is the underworld.[81] At Ugarit, Mot is death personified, and this imagery seems to have penetrated the Hebrew Bible.[82] In the Ugaritic texts, Mot rivals fertility. This may be the reason why his name never occurs in the sacrificial lists at Ugarit. Rather, we have evidence of the Canaanites continually offering sacrifice to Baal with the anticipation that he will conquer Mot.[83]

In the mythic texts, Mot is depicted as a dreadful monster with a large mouth and a hunger that is never satisfied.[84] Mot is the god of death and the underworld, and he can even swallow Baal. However, Baal emerges from his grasp in a cyclical fashion, to reign as lord of the earth. Scholars disagree on whether the Baal-Mot epic is to be interpreted as a sabbatical or seasonal cycle.[85] Of this oft-debated issue, Eakin explains that "regardless, Baal was understood as a fertility god operative on a cyclical basis, either seasonal or sabbatical, while Mot was the deity capable of rendering ineffective temporarily Baal's regenerative powers."[86]

This overview of the primary Canaanite deities at Ugarit provides a basic understanding of how Canaanite religion may have functioned. The predominant view held by most scholars is that these Baal texts focus on explaining how Baal became the high god and how the seasonal cycle is maintained.[87] It appears that most sacrifices were intended to perpetuate the cyclical process of nature and that the myths were developed to explain these cycles. Lawrence E. Toombs explains the Baalistic cycle.

> A cyclical understanding of reality lies behind the myth. However the human being and his society are bound up in and controlled by not one cycle but many—the cycle of tides in the ocean (restless Yam attempting to push beyond his limit), the succession of day and night, the annual cycle of seasons, the growth and death of crops, the periodic recurrence of drought followed by seasons of plenty....[88]

Frank Eakin writes of fertility and the cyclic process of nature.

> It was this association, tied to the agrarian pursuit... that led the Canaanites to emulate nature via sex and to encourage thereby their deities to the sexual relationship and consequently assure fertility to crops and flocks. It was this manner of life, built upon completely different cultural presuppositions, that the immigrating Israelites confronted and had to choose whether to combat or consolidate.[89]

The following chapters of this study will demonstrate that the Deuteronomic History supplied the Israelites with polemical literary material, especially dealing with water and storm, in order to fight Baalism rather than to conform to it.

NOTES

1. Mitchell A. Dahood, "Ancient Semitic Deities in Syria and Palestine," in Le Antiche Divinita Semitiche, ed. Sabatino Moscati, in *Studi Semitici* 1 (Centro di Studi Semitici, 1958), 67; James B. Pritchard, *Archaeology and the Old Testament* (London: Princeton University Press, 1958), 107.

2. For the complete account of these excavations, see Claude F. A. Schaeffer, *The Cuneiform Texts of Ras Shamra-Ugarit* (Published for the British Academy by Humphrey Milford Publishers. London: Oxford University Press, 1939).

3. Arvid S. Kapelrud, "Ugarit," in vol. 4 of *The Interpreter's Dictionary of the Bible*, ed. George A. Buttrick, Thomas Samuel Kepler, John Knox, Herbert Gordon May, Samuel Terrein, and Emory Stevens Bucker (Nashville: Abingdon Press, 1982), 725.

4. Paul L. Watson, "Mot, The God of Death at Ugarit and in the Old Testament" (Ph.D. diss., Yale University, 1970), 271.

5. William Jeffree Jobling, "Canaan, Ugarit and the Old Testament: A Study in Relationships" (Ph.D. diss., University of Sydney, Australia, 1976), 981–82.

6. Ibid., 979.

7. William F. Albright, *Yahweh and the Gods of Canaan* (Garden City, N.Y.: Doubleday, 1968), 116.

8. Frank E. Eakin, Jr., *The Religion and Culture of Israel: An Introduction to Old Testament Thought* (Boston: Allyn and Bacon, 1971), 199.

9. Dahood, "Ancient Semitic Deities in Syria and Palestine," 72.

10. Eakin, *The Religion and Culture of Israel*, 199.

11. See Dahood, "Ancient Semitic Deities in Syria and Palestine," 69.

12. James B. Pritchard, *Palestinian Figurines in Relation to Certain Goddesses Known through Literature*, ed. Zellig S. Harris, American

Oriental Series 24 (New Haven, Conn.: American Oriental Society, 1943), 87.

13. For an excellent discussion of this subject, see Beatrice A. Brooks, "Fertility Cult Functionaries in the Old Testament," *Journal of Biblical Literature* 60 (1941): 227–53.

14. Walter C. Kaiser, Jr., "The Ugaritic Pantheon" (Ph.D. diss., Brandeis University, 1973), 48.

15. Ibid.

16. Asherah occurs both in the masculine plural as Asherim and in the feminine plural as Asheroth. J. C. De Moor, "'asherah," in vol. 2 of *Theological Dictionary of the Old Testament*, ed. G. Johannes Botterweck and Helmer Ringgren, trans. John T. Willis (Grand Rapids, Mich.: William B. Eerdsman Publishing Co., 1986), 439.

17. For a more complete treatise on the goddess Asherah in the Old Testament, see John Day, "Asherah in the Hebrew Bible and Northwest Semitic Literature," *Journal of Biblical Literature* 105 (September 1986): 395–408. For a discussion of the possible relationship between Asherah and Yahweh, see Richard J. Petty, "Asherah: Goddess of Israel" (Ph.D. diss., Marquette University, 1985).

18. Ulf Oldenburg, *The Conflict between El and Ba'al in Canaanite Religion* (Leiden: E. J. Brill, 1969), 117.

19. For an excellent treatise on the issue of Asherah as both a proper name as well as a cultic object, see Day, "Asherah in the Hebrew Bible and Northwest Semitic Literature."

20. Francis Brown, S. R. Driver, and C. A. Briggs, *A Hebrew and English Lexicon of the Old Testament* (Oxford: Clarendon Press, 1951), 81.

21. Day, "Asherah in the Hebrew Bible and Northwest Semitic Literature," 403.

22. The stipulation to burn the pole indicates that the cultic object was probably a wooden post. There is no archaeological evidence to confirm this idea because wood is perishable.

23. Dahood, "Ancient Semitic Deities in Syria and Palestine," 80.

24. Arvid S. Kapelrud, *The Violent Goddess Anat in the Ras Shamra Texts* (Oslo: Universitetsforlaget, 1969), 114–15.

25. Ibid., 114.

26. William F. Albright, *Archaeology and the Religion of Israel* (Baltimore: Johns Hopkins Press, 1942), 195 n. 14.

27. Kaiser, "The Ugaritic Pantheon," 153.

28. Ibid., 155.

29. Josh. 19:38; Judg. 1:33.

30. Josh. 21:18; 1 Kings 2:26; 1 Chron. 6:60; 7:8; Ezra 2:23; Neh. 7:27; 10:19; 11:32; Isa. 10:30; Jer. 1:1; 11:21, 23; 29:27; 32:7–9.

31. Kapelrud, *The Violent Goddess Anat in the Ras Shamra Texts*, 10–11.

32. Kaiser, "The Ugaritic Pantheon," 165.

33. Ibid., 38.

34. John Gray, "Ashtoreth," in vol. 1 of *The Interpreter's Dictionary of the Bible*, ed. George A. Buttrick, Thomas Samuel Kepler, John Knox, Herbert Gordon May, Samuel Terrein, and Emory Stevens Bucker (Nashville: Abingdon Press, 1982), 255.

35. Ibid.

36. Albright, *Archaeology and the Religion of Israel*, 74.

37. Eakin, *The Religion and Culture of Israel*, 204.

38. Marvin J. Pope, "El in the Ugaritic Texts," in vol. 2 of *Supplements to Vetus Testamentum*, ed. G. W. Anderson, P. A. H. De Boer, Millar Burrows, Henri Cazelles, E. Hammershaimb, and Martin Noth (Leiden: E. J. Brill, 1955), 1.

39. Ibid., 6.

40. Kaiser, "The Ugaritic Pantheon," 21.

41. Ibid., 22–27.

42. Ibid., 82.

43. William F. Albright, review of *El in the Ugaritic Texts*, by Marvin J. Pope, *Journal of Biblical Literature* 75 (1956): 255.

44. Dahood, "Ancient Semitic Deities in Syria and Palestine," 78.

45. John Gray, "The Legacy of Canaan. The Ras Shamra Texts and Their Relevance to the Old Testament," in vol. 5 of *Supplements to Vetus Testamentum*, ed. G. W. Anderson, P. A. H. De Boer, Millar Burrows, Henri Cazelles, E. Hammershaimb, and Martin Noth (Leiden: E. J. Brill, 1957), 120.

46. Schaeffer, *The Cuneiform Texts of Ras Shamra-Ugarit*, 8.

47. Ibid., 116.

48. Pope, "El in the Ugaritic Texts," 103–4.

49. Other scholars who share Pope's view on this point are Arvid S. Kapelrud, *Baal in the Ras Shamra Texts* (Copenhagen: G. E. C. Gad Publisher, 1952); Gray, *The Legacy of Canaan*, 1957; and Oldenburg, *The Conflict between El and Ba'al in Canaanite Religion*, 1969.

50. Marvin H. Pope, "The Status of El at Ugarit," *Ugarit-Forschungen* 19 (1987): 229.

51. There are three major works on the storm god Baal-Hadad: Hans Martin Scholbies, "Der akkadische Wettergott in Mesopotamien" (Ph.D. diss., Philosophische Fakultät der Friedrich-Wilhelm-Universität zu Berlin, 1925); Kapelrud, *Baal In The Ras Shamra Texts*; and most recently, Hassan S. Haddad, "Baal-Hadad: A Study of the Syrian Storm-God" (Ph.D. diss., University of Chicago, 1960).

52. Oldenburg, *The Conflict between El And Ba'al In Canaanite Religion*, 57–58.

53. Ibid., 58.

54. Ibid.

55. Ibid., 59.

56. J. C. De Moor, "ba'al," in vol. 2 of _Theological Dictionary of the Old Testament_, ed. G. Johannes Botterweck and Helmer Ringgren, trans. John T. Willis (Grand Rapids, Mich.: William B. Eerdsman Publishing Co., 1986), 183.

57. Harvey H. Guthrie, Jr., "Hadad," in vol. 2 of _The Interpreter's Dictionary of the Bible_, ed. George A. Buttrick, Thomas Samuel Kepler, John Knox, Herbert Gordon May, Samuel Terrein, and Emory Stevens Bucker (Nashville: Abingdon Press, 1982), 507.

58. J. C. L. Gibson, "The Theology of the Ugaritic Baal Cycle," _Orientalia_ 53 (1984): 202–19, fasc. #2.

59. Arvid S. Kapelrud, _The Ras Shamra Discoveries and the Old Testament_, trans. G. W. Anderson (Norman: University of Oklahoma, 1963), 14.

60. Kaiser, "The Ugaritic Pantheon," 55.

61. De Moor, "ba'al," 187–88.

62. M. J. Mulder, "Baal in the Old Testament," in vol. 2 of _Theological Dictionary of the Old Testament_, ed. G. Johannes Botterweck and Helmer Ringgren, trans. John T. Willis (Grand Rapids, Mich: William B. Eerdsman Publishing Co., 1986), 197.

63. Ibid., 193–94.

64. Oldenburg. _The Conflict between El and Ba'al in Canaanite Religion_, 1.

65. Kapelrud, _Baal in the Ras Shamra Texts_, 52.

66. Ibid., 65.

67. Dahood, "Ancient Semitic Deities in Syria and Palestine," 78–79.

68. Oldenburg, _The Conflict between El and Ba'al In Canaanite Religion_, 184.

69. Ibid., 54.

70. Ibid., 44ff.

71. Ibid., 47.

72. Kapelrud, *Baal in the Ras Shamra Texts*, 54.

73. Kaiser, "The Ugaritic Pantheon," 74.

74. Schaeffer, *The Cuneiform Texts of Ras Shamra-Ugarit*, 8.

75. For evidence of Dagon in the Hebrew Bible, see 1 Sam. 5:2–7; 31:10; and Judg. 16:23.

76. Kaiser, "The Ugaritic Pantheon," 108–9. For more information regarding the god Yam, see pp. 108–13.

77. Theodore H. Gaster, *Thespis: Ritual, Myth, and Drama in the Ancient Near East*, rev. ed. (New York: Gordian Press, 1975), 125.

78. Kaiser, "The Ugaritic Pantheon," 111–12. See also Gaster, *Thespis*, 186; and Kapelrud, *Baal in the Ras Shamra Texts*, 102, who maintain that Yam and Lotan are identical.

79. For an exhaustive treatment of all passages dealing with the issue of the divine combat between Yahweh and the sea or sea serpent, see John Day, *God's Conflict with the Dragon and the Sea: Echoes of a Canaanite Myth in the Old Testament* (Cambridge: Cambridge University Press, 1985), 214–20.

80. Lawrence E. Toombs, "Baal, Lord of the Earth: The Ugaritic Epic," in *The Word of the Lord Will Go Forth: Essays in Honor of D. N. Freedman*, ed. Carol L. Meyers and Michael O'Connor (Winona Lake, Ind.: Published for A.S.O.R. by Eisenbrauns, 1983), 618.

81. Kaiser, "The Ugaritic Pantheon," 136.

82. For a more detailed study of the god Mot and his imagery in the Hebrew Bible, see Watson, "Mot, The God of Death at Ugarit and in the Old Testament."

83. Oldenburg, *The Conflict between El and Ba'al in Canaanite Religion*, 38–39.

84. Ibid., 36.

85. These opinions will be dealt with at greater length in the discussion of the text of 1 Sam. 12:17–18.

86. Eakin, *The Religion and Culture of Israel*, 203.

87. Mark S. Smith, "Interpreting the Baal Cycle," *Ugaritic-Forschungen* 18 (1986): 313, maintains, however, that there are five different interpretations on this subject: (1) Seasonal, (2) Ritual, (3) Cosmogonic, (4) Struggle of life vs. death, and (5) Kingship.

88. Toombs, "Baal, Lord of the Earth: The Ugaritic Epic," 621.

89. Eakin, *The Religion And Culture Of Israel*, 200.

CHAPTER 2

DEUTERONOMY AND THE DEUTERONOMIC HISTORY

This chapter begins with a definition of the Deuteronomic History, followed by a discussion of the general polemics against Baalism within this history. The specific role of the Book of Deuteronomy within the Deuteronomic History is then addressed. The Book of Deuteronomy is then analyzed in relation to its authorship, date, structure, style, and content. Finally, the polemics against Baalism are viewed within the covenantal context of the Book of Deuteronomy.

THE DEUTERONOMIC HISTORY

In 1943 Martin Noth initially proposed the thesis of a Deuteronomic History.[1] Noth argued that a single exilic historian or author developed the stratum of text in the Hebrew Bible from Deuteronomy through Kings. He organized and edited materials he collected aimed at a theological explanation for the fall of Israel.[2] This history is called "Deuteronomic" or "Deuteronomistic" because the Book of Deuteronomy serves as the general standard for the writer's interpretation of history.[3]

Much like Wellhausen's documentary hypothesis, Noth's thesis has gained significant attention in biblical scholarship. However, as with Wellhausen's model, there have been those who have modified Noth's theory as well as those who utterly reject his claim.[4] The most palatable position is that the Deuteronomic History (hereafter referred to as DH) was arranged and edited by people identified by the term "Deuteronomist" (hereafter referred to as DTR), who, through their combined efforts, function as the implied writer of this work in an authorial or editorial role.

The major editorial work of DTR seems to occur in the era of Josiah's reformation, the final editing taking place in the exilic period.[5] However, this work does not focus on a discussion of the DH hypothesis.[6] Scholars have generally accepted the theory of a Deuteronomic History as the corpus of literature in Deuteronomy through Kings because of the abundant literary evidence suggesting a uniformity in this stratum of the Hebrew Bible.

The major concern of DTR in the composition of the DH is "a theological interpretation of the catastrophe which befell the two kingdoms."[7] Although John Van Seters may be right when he argues that "all Hebrew historiography is written from a theological perspective,"[8] this is especially true in the DH, where the history reaches a climax of moralistic interpretation.[9] Christopher North suggests that "history as written by the Deuteronomists was 'history with a purpose.' Never have historians been more didactic, or so concerned to point the moral for their contemporaries. Their style is hortatory and sermonic, and can easily be recognized even in translation."[10]

Within the DH, a central concern is idolatry. Yahweh strongly forbids Israel to worship the false gods of other nations. This is especially true of the Canaanite gods, which Israel is commanded to eliminate completely.[11] Eakin is correct in maintaining that as DTR reflected upon the Israelite history, the one issue of critical concern was the struggle against Baalism.[12] Eakin explains:

> ...when the final edition of the Deuteronomic history
> was completed, the one thing of which the Israelites
> were certain was that the constant apostasy to Baalism,
> had been a major factor in leading to their present
> predicament. With this in mind, a fervent literary
> attack was made upon Baalism.[13]

Throughout the Hebrew Bible, Baalism is often viewed through Yahwistic lenses. This is especially apparent in the DH, in which a polemical perception against Baal is magnified. The reason for this is that the Baal cult practiced alongside Yahwism necessitated a polemic.[14]

DEUTERONOMY

Although the Book of Deuteronomy forms an integral part of the DH, it is also considered a separate entity within this corpus. Noth maintains that "Josh.-Kings forms an independent work, with the Book of Deuteronomy added to it as a kind of paradigmatic prologue."[15] Robert Polzin expands this view when he states the following:

> In Deuteronomy, reported speech of its hero [Moses] is emphasized, in Joshua-2 Kings, the reporting speech of it's narrator is dominant. It is as though the Deuteronomist is telling us in Deuteronomy, "Here is what God has prophesied concerning Israel," but in Joshua-2 Kings, "This is how God's word has been exactly fulfilled in Israelite history from the settlement to the destruction of Jerusalem and the Exile."[16]

McCarter concludes, "Deuteronomism was a style of theology that drew its major tenets from the teachings of the Book of Deuteronomy. It stressed centralization of worship in Jerusalem, obedience to Deuteronomic law, and avoidance of any kind of apostasy, all according to a rigid system of reward and punishment."[17] Thus the Book of Deuteronomy serves not only as an introduction to the DH, but also as a standard to be followed by the remaining literature in the Deuteronomic corpus.

Scholars have debated for centuries the authorship of the Book of Deuteronomy. Theories of authorship by individuals such as Samuel and especially Moses have been advanced, along with theories of groups of people such as levitical priests, prophetic circles, or the Jerusalem priesthood.[18] Concerning the latter, Patrick D. Miller writes,

> It is rare that one can say precisely who wrote a biblical book. That is certainly the case with the Book of Deuteronomy. A history of composition stretching over a hundred years or more...would obviously make the identity of a particular author moot. The question of who wrote the book, therefore, has to be reformulated to ask, rather, what circles or groups of persons might have been responsible for formulating, collecting, editing, and expanding the work before us.[19]

Although the identity of the specific author remains generally unknown to scholars at large,[20] Miller offers some major proposals. He admits that while many propositions are available, three major proposals stand out in addressing this question.[21] The first, proposed by E. W. Nicholson, is that the book was composed by prophetic circles.[22] A second theory, suggested by Gerhard von Rad, is that Deuteronomy developed in Levitical priestly circles.[23] A third proposal, suggested by Moshe Weinfeld, maintains that Deuteronomy was composed by wisdom and scribal circles.[24]

The dating of the text has also undergone careful scrutiny, and scholars are more agreed on this question than they are on the authorship. In 1805 W. M. L. De Wette advocated that the Book of Deuteronomy was definitely related to Josiah's reform (621 B.C.) and that it was at least in part a composition of Josiah's period. P. C. Craigie remarks that

> in more recent studies, Deuteronomy is viewed not simply as a product of the seventh century; rather it is thought to be a composition of very much older traditions, which have nevertheless, been reworked in the period of the reform.[25]

E. W. Nicholson agrees that its final composition is connected to Josiah's reform and thus observes that the widely-held view is that the book was composed in the seventh century B.C.[26]

This argument is largely based on the evidence that a book uncovered at the temple in the days of King Josiah was in some way related to the Book of Deuteronomy (see 2 Kgs. 22:8). H. H. Rowley suggests "that Josiah's law book was Deuteronomy in some form, though not wholly identified with the present book of Deuteronomy, seems to be one of the most firmly established results of Old Testament scholarship."[27]

Although most scholars will readily admit to certain evidence of late composition, there is also strong evidence that such a composition rested upon traditions much earlier than the Josianic era. However, the precise date of these early materials is uncertain.[28]

The stylistic structure of the Book of Deuteronomy is unique in format. Patrick Miller proposes "that an explicit literary structure to the book is expressed in the sermons of Moses; a substructure is discernible in the covenantal character of the book; and a theological structure is revealed in its theme of the exclusive worship of the Lord."[29] Each of these three elements deserves careful consideration.

To understand the explicit literary structure of the book requires study of the first sentence of its introductory verse: "These are the words that Moses addressed to all Israel on the other side of the Jordan" (Deut. 1:1).[30] This verse, which denotes obvious editing, portrays a setting wherein Moses becomes the book's authoritative author. "The immediate hero of the book is Moses as the spokesman of God. The only other person quoted by the narrator is God," writes Robert Polzin.[31] Moses preaches the law of Yahweh to Israel as they are on the threshold of entering the promised land. What follows is a series of Mosaic speeches. Norbert Lohfink infers "the book is a kind of archive, an orderly collection of speeches organized around a system of four titles: 1:1; 4:44; 29:1; [H 28:69]; 33:1." Lohfink identifies four "Mosaic texts" and divides them as follows:

> 1–4, a speech of Moses... 5–28, the law or the teachings of Moses... 29–32, the ritual text of covenant-making in Moab... 33, the blessing of Moses. Further, the first three texts (except ch. 32) are presented in typical Deuteronomic prose: the fourth is poetic.[32]

The law code (Deut. 5–28) occupies the largest portion of this division. R. E. Clements highlights a key feature of the literary structure of the text, noting that "whereas the figure of Moses is largely absent from the law code, it completely dominates the framework."[33] This suggests the framework was composed by DTR. In fact, von Rad does propose that Deuteronomy 1–4 and Deuteronomy 31–34 are to be assigned to the Deuteronomic historians.[34] Martin Noth goes a step farther in maintaining that Deuteronomy 1–4 and Deuteronomy 31 and 34 are also to be viewed as an introduction to the DH.[35] Noth sees Deuteronomy 32 (the song of Moses) and Deuteronomy 33 (the blessing of Moses) as later insertions by DTR.[36]

Perhaps a Mosaic structure is emphasized in Deuteronomy as well as the DH because Moses was traditionally associated with the law. Further, at the time of their editorial composition, DTR recognized a great need for Israel to return to the law and therefore provided themselves with an authoritative framework. Patrick Miller notes that "mosaic speech is a literary and theological device used by the Deuteronomist to speak centuries later in an authoritative manner to the people of his own day."[37] The Josianic reforms of the seventh century certainly hint at a time of such a need.

As mentioned, the law book (Deut. 5–28) occupies the greatest portion of the Book of Deuteronomy and provides us with a covenantal substructure. Lohfink writes that "it becomes clear that Deut. 5–28 is to be understood as the textual basis of a contract between Yahweh and the people of Israel."[38] Such a contract is a covenant theology and cannot be fully understood without a comparative analysis to ancient Near Eastern vassal treaties.[39]

In the 1950s George E. Mendenhall asserted a resemblance between the Hittite suzerainty vassal treaties (dated 1450–1200 B.C) and the Israelite law and covenant.[40] In 1972 Moshe Weinfeld pointed out that Mendenhall had reached his conclusions only in relation to the covenants at Shechem and Sinai in Exodus 19–24. Weinfeld stressed that Mendenhall had not investigated whether such a similarity existed between the Hittite treaties and the later material in the Book of Deuteronomy. He also suggested that Mendenhall had probably not considered the Near Eastern treaties dated from the ninth to the seventh centuries B.C. as he had the earlier Hittite treaties, because of their poor fragmentary condition. Weinfeld maintained that Mendenhall's conclusions (that the Hittite treaties are unique and served as the sole prototype for Israel's covenant law) have been proven false because of the discovery of treaties made between Esarhaddon and his eastern vassals in 672 B.C.: these treaties were found about two years after his publications. Furthermore, Weinfeld advanced the idea that the traditional Near Eastern treaty structure did not change from the period of the Hittite vassal treaty to the time of the neo–Assyrian period. Finally, Weinfeld concluded that on the basis of this evidence, it is more likely that the covenant material in the Book of Deuteronomy resembles the contemporary Assyrian vassal treaties of the seventh century, rather than the Hittite vassal treaties dated much earlier.[41]

Weinfeld has not had the last word on this issue. Thirty years after Mendenhall's pioneer research and many years following Weinfeld's remarks, Mendenhall again treated the topic of the Hittite suzerainty vassal treaty and reasserted his former views, in spite of other scholars' research, when he claimed,

> a majority of scholars...have been forced to admit that the book of Deuteronomy certainly does reflect the old suzerainty treaty structure. Unfortunately, these scholars have such negligible historical orientation that they do not even see the historical problems of explaining the sudden resurrection of a structure that had been dead for half a millennium. The fact is the book of Deuteronomy came into existence in association with the "reform" movement of King Josiah, which, of necessity, like all reform movements, was based upon a new valuation and understanding of the remote past. The unknown writers of Deuteronomy had nothing to do with creating ex nihilo that old treaty structure: they returned to the past for traditions that had been contemptuously ignored for centuries by the secure politicians of the monarchy.... It is not the first time, and certainly not the last, that modern scholars have

been unable to distinguish between the origin of the important cultural motif and its much later re-discovery and political exploitation.[42]

In any case, Weinfeld and Mendenhall did agree on a statement by J. N. M. Wijngaards: "It will be readily admitted that the code of law (Dtn 5–28) originated in the context of covenantal instruction." Furthermore, to conclude this discussion of the issue of dating, she writes: "The question which remains to be answered is where and when this original code of law was formulated."[43]

Lohfink suggests that the document uncovered in Josiah's day was probably "...identical with an early edition of Deut. 5–28."[44] Notably, in the Hebrew text, this document is called *sepher ha-berit* (book of the covenant) (2 Kgs. 23:2). Concerning the division of this law code, Dennis J. McCarthy writes that "in sum Dt 5–28 consists of the sequence: historical and parenetic introduction [5–11], laws [12–26], blessing and curses [27–28]."[45]

A critical component of the concept of covenant in the Book of Deuteronomy has to do with the issue of land. The promised land of Israel represents Yahweh's gift to his covenant people. "It is the land which is the focus of promise, the land which is either reward for obedience or the place where the law is to be obeyed.... For Deuteronomy life itself means life in the land in covenant with Yahweh,"[46] claimed A. D. H. Mayes. Walter Brueggeman also affirmed that "the gifted land is covenanted land. It is not only nourishing space, it is also covenanted place. The Jordan is entry not into safe place, but into a context of covenant."[47]

In this covenantal context, the Israelites would be tested to see whether they would obey the laws of Yahweh. Although the land was viewed as a reflection of perfection, it was at the same time an environment designed to prove them. 2 Maccabees 5:19 observes, "the Lord did not select the people for the sake of the place, but the place for the sake of the people."

The geography of an area naturally influences the life of the people living there.[48] This is particularly so with the political geography of the covenant land of Israel, the only land that lies at the crossroads of three nations.[49] The geography of the land of Israel was like a stage on which a drama would be played.[50] Israel, which served as a land bridge, was often caught between the cross fire of the nations they feared most, Egypt and Mesopotamia. Palestine's story is a history of Mesopotamia's and Egypt's struggle to control this bridge.[51]

In addition to these nations, Israel also confronted the Canaanite peoples who nestled into the valleys of the land of Canaan. One reason such groups could coexist with each other is attributable to the diverse topography of this land of hills and valleys, caused by the Jordan rift. This 4,000-mile fissure in the earth runs from Syria to Mozambique. It is the largest crack in the surface of the earth. The rift is Israel's most unusual geographic feature, creating many creases in the land that form hills and valleys. Such diverse topography is not found in either Egypt or Mesopotamia, whose lands are mostly flat deserts irrigated by rivers.

The climatic conditions of Israel are also diverse and can be observed today as anciently because these conditions have hardly changed.[52] This diversity is based on the natural setting of the land, which lies between desert and sea. These two opposing forces create a climatic condition that is a unique feature of this land. The sea winds bring moisture from the west, while the desert winds carry dryness from the east.[53]

Israel generally received its moisture through rain in the winter and dew in the summer. However, the climate of the land was not always predictable, especially the rain, and there were sometimes extended periods of drought.[54] Such unstable conditions provide the context for Deuteronomic theology which connected the lack of moisture with a lack of obedience to some point of the covenant. The Deuteronomic law had stipulated that if Israel obeyed the commandments of the Lord (Deut. 28:1), he would provide rain for them in its proper season (Deut. 28:12). The stipulations of the covenant, however, were such that if the Israelites did not obey the laws, they would be cursed (Deut. 28:15). "The skies above your head shall be copper and the earth under you iron. The Lord will make the rain of your land dust, and sand shall drop on you from the sky, until you are wiped out" (Deut. 28:23–24).[55]

The necessity of obedience to the covenant of Yahweh is emphasized throughout the Book of Deuteronomy. For example, the text counsels: "For you are about to cross the Jordan to enter and possess the land that the Lord your God is assigning to you. When you have occupied it and are settled in it, make sure to observe all the laws and rules that I have set before you this day."[56] Thus the price for admission into and occupation of the promised land was obedience to all the stipulations of the covenant of Yahweh. Wijnsgaards also points out that the text carefully portrays the covenantal instruction as taking place *before* the Hebrew tribes crossed the Jordan River.[57]

The Book of Deuteronomy portrays this promised land as a very fertile land, choice above all others: "For the Lord your God is bringing you into a good land, a land with streams and springs and fountains issuing from valleys and hills; a land of wheat and barley, of vines, figs, and pomegranates, a land of olives trees and honey"[58] Miller indicates that the land is the sphere where blessings are promised to the people and that nearly all blessings referenced in Deuteronomy refer to it.[59] The first typification of this sphere is its plentitude of water.

Later in the text we find another vivid description of this unique land and the conditions that Israel must obey to obtain and remain in the land and to have the land continue to provide its fructifying effects throughout the cyclic year. Because this passage is so important to our discussion, a complete translation of Deut. 11:8–17 is provided:

> (8) Keep, therefore, all the instruction that I place upon you today, so that you may have the strength to enter and take possession of the land that you are about to cross into and possess, (9) and that you may long endure upon the soil that the Lord swore to your fathers to assign to them and to their posterity, a land flowing with milk and honey. (10) For the land that you are about to enter and possess is not like the land of Egypt from which you have come. There the grain you sowed had to be watered by your own labors, like a vegetable garden; (11) but the land you are about to cross into and possess, a land of hills and valleys, soaks up its water from the rains of heaven. (12) It is a land which the Lord your God looks after, on which the Lord your God always keeps his eye, from the beginning of the year until the end of the year. (13) If then, you obey the commandments that I enjoin upon you this day, to love the Lord your God and to serve him with all your heart and soul, (14) I will grant the rain for your land in season, the early rain and the later rain. You shall gather in your grain and wine and oil. (15) I will also provide grass in the fields for your cattle, and thus you will eat your fill. (16) Beware not to be lured away to serve other gods and bow to them. (17) For the Lord's anger will be kindled against you, and he will shut up the skies so that there will be no rain and the ground will not yield its produce; and you will

soon perish from the good land that the Lord is
assigning you.

In verses 10–11, the rain water resources of Israel are compared
with the land irrigation of Egypt, of which Jack Shechter observes:

> In Egypt rain is exceedingly rare and crops are
> dependent on the annual inundation of the Nile and
> a system of irrigation.... The land of Israel about to
> be possessed, on the other hand, is a land of hills and
> valleys which draws its water directly from the rains
> of heaven. Thus it is a superior land because its
> sustenance comes directly from God.[60]

In verses 12–14, Yahweh, aware of the conditions that prevail in
his land, promises that his sacred soil will receive the proper amount
of moisture in its proper season when Israel is obedient to the terms
of the covenant. Verse 14 speaks of early and later rains in order to
assure the necessity of a continuous fidelity. Henry H. Shires and
Pierson Parker explained the definition and the particular mention of
these rains.

> The early rain and the later rain, i.e., the fall and
> spring rains in October-November and in March-April.
> While the rainy season extends through the winter, the
> fall and spring rains were usually singled out for
> special mention because the first broke the summer's
> drought and ushered in the plowing season, while the
> second was the last before the summer drought and one
> which brought verdure to the whole countryside.[61]

Verse 15 describes the agricultural produce that will come forth
as a result of the rains upon the fertile soil: grain, wine (grapes), and
oil (olives). Aharoni comments that "agriculture was the basis for the
economy of most countries in antiquity including Palestine....
Palestinian agriculture was mainly natural farming without irrigation."[62]

Verses 16–17 are a specific warning to Israel: They are not to
worship any other god. If they do, the penalty will be no rain, and
therefore they will perish from off the land. In verse 13, Israel was told
to love and serve with all their hearts *only* Yahweh. "The idea that
serving other gods inevitably causes drought and famine is an ancient
biblical notion and it found its classical expression in Deut. 11:16–17."[63]

As the Israelites leave the desert and enter the lavish land of
Canaan, they enter an agricultural territory unknown to them. "One

concern dominates. How will Israel recognize their Lord in their agricultural world? Up to this moment God has revealed himself in the historical events of the exodus-conquest."[64] In their apprehension, as soon as the unpredictable climate arrived, the Israelite farmers appear to have asked their Canaanite neighbors, "How does your garden grow?"

Baly interjects that the most intense temptation of the ancient Israelite farmer was "to placate every power that he had ever heard of, just in case there might be some truth in the story that this or that local deity had got the key to the [water] storehouse."[65] Unlike the Egyptians, who could get more out of the soil by working a little harder with irrigation, Israel had to rely on the moisture of heaven and maximized the rainfall through waterproof, lime-plastered cisterns.[66] Although the farmer's one alternative was to turn to the fertility gods and fertility rituals of the Canaanites, that is precisely the danger against which this passage warns (v. 16).[67] The warning most often went unheeded, and as the Israelites entered Canaan, they embraced the religious practices of the Canaanite culture. The Israelites succumbed to the allure of the Canaanite storm god Baal and drowned in Baalism. This point helps to explain the theological structure of the Book of Deuteronomy, which reflects an emphasis on the theme of an exclusive worship of Yahweh. This theological structure is a catalytic feature of Deuteronomy which affects not only the Deuteronomic corpus, but the entire Hebrew Bible. According to George W. Anderson, "the importance of Deuteronomy in the history of religion can hardly be overestimated. It gathered up some of the best traditions of a Yahwism militant against pagan corruption."[68] The Deuteronomic writers likely recognized the value of these earlier materials which demonstrated a traditional monotheistic view of which they were emphasizing. Yet Clements reminds us that these authors were not just collectors or merely traditionalists: "What they have given us in their book is a highly original and fresh composition; and it is this originality and freshness that mark its great importance for the emergence of the Old Testament."[69] They seek to incorporate the earlier traditions into their own day.[70]

Deuteronomy is central to the issue of strict Yahwistic theology in the Hebrew Bible.[71] It signals the junction where the law ends and the prophets begin and serves as a standard for orthodoxy of Israelite faith.[72] Clements observes that "one of the most striking of all the features of the book of Deuteronomy is the way in which all of the material it contains in both the law code and the framework shows evidence of having been composed in conformity to certain basic theological ideas." Such a theological framework was certainly erected against the influence of Baalism that pervaded Israel. Clements further maintains that "the Deuteronomic authors firmly believed that the national disasters which had overtaken their nation were the consequences of the fact that God's anger had been aroused against the entire nation on account of its indifference to its inherited religious loyalty."[73] Thus it is apparent that Deuteronomy has a monotheistic modality that focuses on the worship of only one God at only one location and strict conformity to the covenant of Yahweh.[74]

The concept of one sanctuary certainly strengthened the belief of one God. It also made it much easier to supervise all that transpired at the Jerusalem temple grounds.[75] The Book of Deuteronomy repeatedly emphasizes this strict command to worship the Lord only at one designated place,[76] and the centralization of worship in one place has always been considered its most unique feature.[77] Yehezkel Kaufmann argues that this unusual feature as well as other peculiarities are found only in Deuteronomy and not in the rest of the Torah: "The stratum of D concerning the centralization of worship must be considered a product of the age in which it first appears as a historical factor, the age of Hezekiah and Josiah. Thus we have a fixed point for the dating of one element of the Torah."[78] Before this legislation, the existence of many altars was tolerated. This stipulation represents an extreme change in the laws and regulations regarding Israel's cultic life.[79]

Clifford informs us that although Israel's legal foundations were similar to those of her neighbors' in the Near East, her perspective on law and covenant were unique. What is most apparent is the Israelite uncompromising concept of monotheism. Israel must conform to the covenantal stipulations and worship only Yahweh and no other gods.[80] The Shema firmly decrees, "Hear O Israel. The Lord is our God, the Lord alone. You shall love the Lord your God with all your heart and with all your soul and with all your might."[81] In this same chapter, Israel is also warned not to worship other gods: "Revere only the Lord your God and worship Him alone, and swear only by His name. Do not follow other gods, any of the gods of the people which are around you. For the Lord your God is a jealous God, lest the anger of the Lord your God blaze forth against you and he wipe you from off the face of the earth." Thus the penalty for worshiping other gods was death.[82] This same punishment was also in force for those who even advocated the worship of other gods.[83]

Clifford again remarks: "In no book of the Bible is exclusive fidelity to the Lord held up so insistently to Israel as it is in Deuteronomy."[84] S. R. Driver maintains that while the Deuteronomic author teaches the fundamental monotheistic message that Yahweh is the sole God, he is at the same time consigned to the "emphatic repudiation" of Baalism.[85] Driver noted that "the encroachments of heathenism formed the pressing danger of the age; and these the author strove to resist by every means of his power."[86] This is very evident from the text, which features an abundance of explicit polemics in which Israel is warned not only not to worship other gods but also to destroy completely all traces of any Baalistic images as well as the Canaanites themselves.[87]

Perhaps the writers of Deuteronomy reasoned that if Israel had obeyed Yahweh by completely destroying the Canaanite cancer of Baalism, she would never have fallen to the illness that resulted in an apostate condition. "This explains the enormous stress throughout Deuteronomy on the danger of fraternizing with the Canaanites. They are to be utterly exterminated, thereby guaranteeing Israel's freedom from their polluting influence," asserts Anthony Phillips.[88]

This stress reflects the setting of Josiah's reformation. Miller argues that this anti-Baalistic emphasis is to be viewed in the context of the late preexilic period.[89] Such an emphasis is surely evidence of an explicit polemic against Baalism. However, there are also polemics of an implicit nature in Deuteronomy which have not been treated adequately, especially in relation to their function in the Deuteronomic History as a whole. These are evidenced particularly in relation to Yahweh's ability to demonstrate his supremacy over the elements of nature, such as his power over the storm and his divine provision of water, dew, and fertility.

Such features can be seen in the poems entitled the Song (Deut. 32) and Blessing (Deut. 33) of Moses, which reveal certain implicit elements that may be viewed as polemics. Each of these poems is an independent composition and both certainly date before the seventh century B.C.[90]

Deuteronomy 32

Otto Eissfeldt dates the Song of Moses to the mid-eleventh century B.C.[91] Albright justifies Eissfeldt's early date on the basis of common archaic vocabulary and morphology in the text and suggests that the

Song of Moses is not to be dated later than the tenth century B.C.[92] David Robertson, who completed a study dealing with the linguistic evidence in dating early Hebrew poetry, also dated this text to the period of the eleventh-tenth centuries B.C. and based his analysis on the archaic morphological characteristics he found as well as the syntactical features.[93]

The Song of Moses begins with a merismus, whereby a plea is made for all to listen to the words of Moses: "Give ear, O heavens and I will speak; hear O earth, the words of my mouth" (Deut. 32:1). The text then utilizes the imagery of moisture. "My knowledge will drop as the rain, my speech shall distil as the dew" (Deut. 32:2). Such imagery suggests that the words of Moses will be productive and accomplish their desired purpose, which is to make known the name of the Lord (Deut. 32:3). The figurative name that Yahweh is given in this text is *ẓur*, "rock" or "cliff." It is used as a figure of God thirty-three times in the Hebrew Bible to symbolize Yahweh's unyielding strength, as well as his defense and support of his chosen people.[94]

Verse 10 indicates that Yahweh found his people Israel in a desert wasteland. Verse 13 denotes that Yahweh provided his people with honey and oil from a rock. The word *ẓur* is used here to refer to the incident when Yahweh through Moses supplied Israel with water as they traveled in the desert.[95] When this story is reviewed in Deuteronomy 8:15, "water," replaces honey and oil.[96] The word pair oil-and-honey bespeaks the divine provision of fertility and life afforded to Israel, much like the phrase "milk and honey" (Deut. 31:20).[97]

These verses assert Yahweh's divine ability to provide for his people. However, such blessings are conditioned on obedience. Yahweh later warns that he will place misfortunes on the disobedient, and states that "I will use up my arrows against them: Wasted by famine and consumed by pestilence" (Deut. 32:23–24). Yahweh's divine protection of Israel from her enemies is then proclaimed:

> When I whet the lightning of my sword, and my hand lays hold of judgment, I will render judgment to mine enemies, and I will deal with those who hate me. I will make my arrows drunk with blood, and my sword shall devour flesh (Deut. 32:41–42).[98]

S. R. Driver maintains that the arrows mentioned in these verses are symbolic of divine chastisement and judgment.[99] Explains H. A. Hoffner: "Yahweh's arrows are often described as being bright; in theopanies, in combination with other storm imagery, they are depicted as lightning."[100] In Habakkuk 3:11 and in 2 Samuel 22:15, the word *ḥeẓ* (arrow) and *baraq* (lightning) are used in parallelism. Thus, one interpretation of the "lightning in the skies" in ancient Israel was viewing them as the arrows of Yahweh.

This image of Yahweh using storm as a weapon against his enemies, whereby Yahweh appropriates Baal motifs, is very apparent in the Deuteronomic History and may be viewed as a polemic against the storm god Baal Hadad as will be demonstrated later in this study. The following inscription is most interesting in this regard as Adad (Hadad) was invoked by Adadnirari in the thirteenth century B.C. in this manner:

> May Adad overwhelm him [the enemy] with an evil downpour, may flood and storm, confusion and tumult,[101] want and famine, drought and hunger, continue in his land... May Adad destroy his land with destructive lightning and cast famine upon his land.[102]

Deuteronomy 33

The orthography of the Blessing of Moses indicates that it was probably written in the tenth century B.C.[103] The majority of this text deals with the blessing Moses is said to have given to each of the tribes of Israel and in this respect is similar to Jacob's blessing of the Israelite tribes as recorded in Genesis 49. In this poem Joseph again receives the superior blessing because he was designated as the birthright son. His blessing in this text includes the promise of proper moisture: dew from above, and the deep from beneath (Deut. 33:13).

The combined blessing of provision and protection is again evidenced in the concluding verses of the text. Driver notes that in Deuteronomy 33:26–29 that "the poet celebrates the fortune of his nation, settled and secure, with the aid of its God, in its *fertile* Palestinian home."[104]

In verse 26 the supremacy of Yahweh is again made manifest with these words: "There is none like the God of Jeshurun, riding through the heavens to help you, the clouds in his majesty."[105] Patrick Miller suggests that this imagery is used to depict Yahweh driving a war chariot into battle.[106]

> The imagery of the divine chariot-cloud motif is indeed of ancient origin and is met with in Ugaritic literature (*rkb ᶜrpt*), which appears to have influenced Biblical

imagery.[107]

This phrase is an epithet for Baal Hadad and is translated as "rider of the clouds." John Day explains that, in this context, *ride* "does not mean that the god is sitting upon a cloud and is thus transported through the air, but rather that he drives his chariot over the skies, the thunder-cloud being mytho-poetically considered as the chariot on which the god stands."[108] Norman C. Habel writes the following concerning the issue of Baal and Yahweh being both depicted as riding the clouds:

> Although there are numerous general references to Yahweh's agitation of the elements of the weather and His overpowering presence in the phenomena of the storms and tempest, the application of the particular epithet, "Rider of the Clouds" to Yahweh the God of Israel, can hardly be accidental. This is the precise title applied to Baal in Canaanite mythology, a title which is used to express a distinctive characteristic of Baal in a culture contemporaneous with that of Israel. This evidence suggests that the relevant passages may reflect a conscious religious polemic against Baal both in the borrowing of Baal's distinctive title as the storm god "who rides the clouds" and in the application of similar storm imagery to the advent of Yahweh from the heavens. The points of the similarity in the storm theophany are obvious.[109]

This imagery reflects the message that Yahweh has displaced Baal as Lord of the storm. In Deuteronomy 33:27 the protective power of Yahweh against the enemies of Israel again surfaces. "The eternal God is your refuge, from beneath are the everlasting arms; and he will drive out the enemy from before you; and he will say, destroy." The next verse merges the theme of protective power and provision into one thought: "Israel will dwell in safety alone, the fountain of Jacob will be upon a land of grain and wine; also his heavens will drop down dew" (Deut. 33:28). It is Yahweh and not Baal Hadad who controls the water supply in the promised land. Once again the imagery of security and proper moisture asserts Yahweh's potency and benevolence towards Israel. Verse 29 cries aloud, "Happy are you Israel, who is like you?"

These poems emphasize Yahweh's divine capabilities of provision through moisture and power through the medium of storm against those who oppose him. These Yahwistic capabilities are utilized by DTR in the remaining body of the Deuteronomic corpus (Joshua-Kings) as implicit polemics against Baal Hadad, the supposed god of water and storm. A textual analysis dealing with the evidence that supports this claim, now follows.

NOTES

1. For a detailed treatment of Noth's theory, see Martin Noth, "The Deuteronomic History," in *Journal for the Study of the Old Testament*, Supplemental Series 15, ed. D. J. A. Clines, P. R. Davies, and D. M. Gunn (Sheffield: JSOT Press, 1981).

2. P. Kyle McCarter, Jr., *I Samuel: A New Translation with Introduction, Notes and Commentary*, vol. 8 of *The Anchor Bible*, ed. W. F. Albright and D. N. Freedman (Garden City, N.Y.: Doubleday, 1984), 14–15.

3. Gerhard von Rad, "The Deuteronomistic Theology of History in the Book of Kings," in *Studies in Deuteronomy*, no. 9 of Studies in Biblical Theology Series, trans. David Stalker (London: SCM Press, 1953), 75.

4. For example, Georg Fohrer adamantly argues, "There never was a Deuteronomic History as a unified literary entity; instead we gave a series of books Deuteronomy-Kings, each composed or edited in a different way." See *Introduction to the Old Testament*, 10th ed., trans. David. E. Green (Nashville: Abingdon Press, 1968), 195.

5. My position is most similar to that of Frank Moore Cross, who maintains that there are two editions of DH: the primary edition in Josiah's era; and the secondary edition, which he dates to the exilic date of 550 B.C. For a more detailed treatment of this theory, see Frank Moore Cross, *Canaanite Myth and Hebrew Epic* (Cambridge: Harvard University Press, 1973), 274–89.

6. For a detailed analysis of the different theories surrounding the Deuteronomic History, see Mark O'Brien, *The Deuteronomistic History Hypothesis: A Reassessment* (Fribourg: Editions Universitaires, 1989).

7. von Rad, "The Deuteronomistic Theology of History in the Book of Kings," 77.

8. John Van Seters, *In Search of History: Historiography in the Ancient World and the Origins of Biblical History* (New Haven, Conn.: Yale University Press, 1983), 361.

9. George Mendenhall, "The Suzerainty Treaty Structure: Thirty Years Later," in *Religion and Law: Biblical-Judaic and Islamic Perspectives*, ed. Edwin B. Firmage, Bernard G. Weiss, and John W. Welch (Winona Lake, Ind.: Eisenbrauns, 1990), 93.

10. Christopher R. North, *The Old Testament Interpretation* (London: Epworth Press, 1953), 92.

11. Aage Bentzen, *Introduction to the Old Testament*, 2 vols. (Copenhagen: G. E. C. Gads, 1949), 1:42–43.

12. Frank E. Eakin, Jr., "The Relationship between Yahwism and Baalism during the Pre-Exilic Period" (Ph.D. diss., Duke University, 1964), 181.

13. Eakin, *The Religion and Culture Of Israel*, 214–15.

14. A. H. W. Curtis, "The 'Subjugation of the Water' Motif in the Psalms: Imagery or Polemic?" *Journal of Semitic Studies* 24 (Autumn 1978): 256.

15. J. R. Porter, "Old Testament Historiography," in *Tradition and Interpretation*, ed. G. W. Anderson (Oxford: Clarendon Press, 1979), 132.

16. Robert Polzin, "Reporting Speech in the Book of Deuteronomy: Toward a Compositional Analysis of the Deuteronomic History," in *Tradition in Transformation: Turning Points in Biblical Faith*, ed. B. Halpern and Jon D. Levenson (Winona Lake, Ind.: Eisenbrauns, 1981), 194–95.

17. McCarter, "I Samuel," 14.

18. E. W. Nicholson, *Deuteronomy and Tradition* (Philadelphia: Fortress Press, 1967), 37.

19. Patrick D. Miller, "Deuteronomy," in *Interpretation: A Bible Commentary for Teaching and Preaching*, ed. James Luther Mays, Patrick D. Miller, Jr., and Paul J. Achtemeier (Louisville, Ky.: John Knox Press, 1990), 5.

20.This author's opinion is the Moses should be considered as the primary source from which the traditions in the Book of Deuteronomy are derived. However, obvious editing has taken place which is readily apparent in the first and last chapters.

21. Ibid.

22. Ibid. For a complete treatise of this theory, see Nicholson, *Deuteronomy and Tradition*.

23. Miller, "Deuteronomy," 6. For a complete discussion of this proposal, see Gerhard von Rad, *Studies in Deuteronomy* (Chicago: Henry Regnery Co., 1953).

24. Miller, "Deuteronomy," 7. For an entire treatise of this hypothesis see, Moshe Weinfeld, *Deuteronomy and the Deuteronomic School* (Oxford: Clarendon Press, 1972).

25. Peter C. Craigie, "The Book of Deuteronomy," in *The New International Commentary in the Old Testament*, ed. R. K. Harrison (Grand Rapids, Mich.: William B. Eerdsman Publishing Co., 1976), 73.

26. Nicholson, *Deuteronomy and Tradition*, 1.

27. H. H. Rowley, *Men of God* (London: Nelson, 1963), 161.

28. Norbert Lohfink, "Deuteronomy," in supplementary volume of *The Interpreter's Dictionary of the Bible*, ed. George A. Buttrick, Thomas Samuel Kepler, John Knox, Herbert Gordon May, Samuel Terrein, and Emory Stevens Bucker (Nashville: Abingdon Press, 1982), 229. Note: This is especially true of the strata of text in Deuteronomy 5–28. Yehezkel Kaufmann, *The Religion of Israel: From Its Beginning to the Babylonian Exile*, trans. Moshe Greenberg (New York: Schocken Books, 1972), 174.

29. Miller, "Deuteronomy," 10.

30. The actual name of the book of Deuteronomy as it is attested in the Hebrew Bible is *elleh ha devarim*. This is taken from the first clause of the first sentence of this book, translated as previously noted, "These are the words..." The name Deuteronomy derives from a misunderstanding of Deut. 17:8 from the Septuagint. The Hebrew words *mishneh* in

this verse would be better translated as "copy"; instead the word was rendered as "second" and so understood in the sense of "second law"; and thus we have the Greek name *Deuteronomy*, meaning second law.

31. Robert Polzin, *Moses and the Deuteronomist: A Literary Study of the Deuteronomistic History, Part One—Deuteronomy, Joshua, Judges* (New York: Seabury Press, 1980), 26.

32. Lohfink, "Deuteronomy," 229.

33. R. E. Clements, "Deuteronomy," in *Old Testament Guides*, ed. R. N. Whybray (Sheffield: JSOT Press, 1989), 33.

34. Gerhard von Rad, "Deuteronomy: A Commentary," in *The Old Testament Library*, ed. G. E. Wright, John Bright, James Barr, and Peter Ackroyd, trans. Dorothea Barton (Philadelphia: Westminster Press, 1966), 12.

35. Noth, "The Deuteronomic History," 13–14.

36. Ibid., 35.

37. Miller, "Deuteronomy," 11–12.

38. Lohfink, "Deuteronomy," 229.

39. Ibid., 231.

40. The accumulation of this research may be found in two articles: George E. Mendenhall, "Ancient Oriental and Biblical Law," *Biblical Archaeologist* 17 (May 1954): 26–46 and "Covenant Forms in Israelite Tradition," *Biblical Archaeologist* 17 (September 1954): 50–76.

41. Weinfeld, *Deuteronomy and the Deuteronomic School*, 58–59.

42. Mendenhall, "The Suzerainty Treaty Structure," 96.

43. J. N. S. Wijngaards, *The Dramatization of Salvific History in the Deuteronomic Schools* (Leiden: E. J. Brill, 1969), 20. Against this view see A. D. H. Mayes, "Deuteronomy," in *New Century Bible Commentary*, ed. R. E. Clements and Matthew Black (Grand Rapids, Mich.: William B. Eerdsman Publishing Co., 1981). Mayes writes: "There is no indication of an association of the original Deuteronomy with covenant

thought" (81). Additionally, Mayes offers no convincing proof for such a statement.

44. Lohfink, "Deuteronomy," 231.

45. Dennis J. McCarthy, *Treaty and Covenant: A Study in Form in the Ancient Oriental Documents and in the Old Testament* (Rome: Biblical Institute Press, 1978), 159.

46. Mayes, "Deuteronomy," 81.

47. Walter Brueggeman, *The Land. Place as Gift, Promise and Challenge in Biblical Faith* (Philadelphia: Fortress Press, 1977), 52–53.

48. Yohanan Aharoni, *The Land of the Bible: A Historical Geography*, trans. and ed. A. F. Rainey (Philadelphia: Westminster Press, 1979), 3.

49. Ibid.

50. Dennis Baly, *The Geography of the Bible* (New York: Harper & Row, 1957), 125.

51. Dennis Baly, *The Geography of the Bible*, rev. ed. (New York: Harper & Row, 1974), 7.

52. R. B. Y. Scott, "Palestine Climate," in vol. 3 of *The Interpreter's Dictionary of the Bible*, ed. George A. Buttrick, Thomas Samuel Kepler, John Knox, Herbert Gordon May, Samuel Terrein, and Emory Stevens Bucker (Nashville: Abingdon Press, 1953), 625.

53. Aharoni, *The Land of the Bible*, 8.

54. Baly, *The Geography of the Bible*, 77.

55. For a parallel to this specific curse, see the Vassal-Treaties of Esarhaddon dating to the late seventh century. In column vi, lines 440-441, as translated by D. J. Wiseman, we read: "[May Adad, controller of the waters of heaven and earth (dry up) your ponds...]" ("The Vassal-Treaties of Esarhaddon," *Iraq* 20 [1958]: 62). He also translates column vii, lines 530-533, which read as follows: "Just as rain does not fall from a brazen heaven, so may rain and dew not come

upon your fields and your meadows; may it rain burning coals instead of dew on your head" (Ibid., 70).

56. Deut. 11:31–32.

57. Wijnsgaards, *The Dramatization of Salvific History in the Deuteronomic Schools*, 22. Here Wijnsgaards supplies a complete list of all the passages in Deuteronomy that specify the stipulations of the covenant that the Israelites received prior to their crossing of the Jordan.

58. Deut. 8:7–8.

59. Miller, "Deuteronomy," 48.

60. Jack Shechter, "The Theology of the Land of Deuteronomy" (Ph.D. diss., University of Michigan, 1985), 100.

61. Henry H. Shires and Pierson Parker, "The Book of Deuteronomy," in vol. 2 of *The Interpreter's Bible*, ed. George A. Buttrick, Walter Russell Bowie, Paul Scherer, John Knox, Samuel Terrein, and Nolan B. Harmon (Nashville: Abingdon Press, 1953), 405.

62. Aharoni, *The Land of the Bible*, 13.

63. Raphael Patai, "The 'Control of Rain' in Ancient Palestine: A Study in Comparative Religion," *Hebrew Union College Annual* 14 (1939): 267.

64. Richard Clifford, "Deuteronomy with an Excursus on Covenant and Law," in vol. 4 of *Old Testament Message: A Biblical Theological Commentary*, ed. C. Stuhlmueller, C. P. McNamara, and M. McNamara (Wilmington, Del.: Michael Glazier, 1982), 66.

65. Baly, *The Geography of the Bible*, 80.

66. Chester C. McCown, "Cistern," *The Interpreter's Dictionary of the Bible* 1:631.

67. David F. Payne, *Deuteronomy* (Philadelphia: Westminster Press, 1985), 75.

68. George W. Anderson, *A Critical Introduction to the Old Testament* (London: Gerald Duckworth & Co., 1959), 44.

69. R. E. Clements, *Deuteronomy* (Sheffield: Academic Press, 1989), 16.

70. von Rad, "Deuteronomy: A Commentary," 23.

71. A. D. H. Mayes, *The Story of Israel between Settlement and Exile: A Redactional Study of the Deuteronomistic History* (London: SCM Press, 1983), vii.

72. Clements, *Deuteronomy*, 95.

73. Ibid., 49, 55.

74. Mayes, "Deuteronomy," 57–58.

75. Clements, *Deuteronomy*, 61.

76. See, for example, Deut. 12:5, 11, 13–14, 18, 21, 26; 14:23–25; 15:20; 16:2, 6, 15–16; 17:8, 10; 18:6.

77. von Rad, "Deuteronomy," 831.

78. Kaufmann, *The Religion of Israel*, 174.

79. Clements, *Deuteronomy*, 60.

80. Clifford, "Deuteronomy with an Excursus on Covenant and Law," 186.

81. Deut. 6:4–5. See also Deut.4:35, 39; 5:2.

82. Deut. 6:13–15. See also Deut. 7:2–5; 8:19–20; 11:16–17; 29:24–27; 30:17–18; 31:16–17.

83. Deut. 13:6-10.

84. Clifford, "Deuteronomy with an Excursus on Covenant and Law," 1.

85. S. R. Driver, *A Critical and Exegetical Commentary on Deuteronomy*, vol. 5 of *The International Critical Commentary*, ed. S. R. Driver, Alfred Plummer, and Charles A. Briggs (New York: Charles Scribner's Sons, 1895), xxvii–xxviii.

86. Ibid., xxxi.

87. Deut. 7:1–5.

88. Anthony Phillips, "Deuteronomy," in *The Cambridge Commentary in the New English Bible*, ed. P. R. Ackroyd, A. R. C. Leaney, and J. W. Packer (Cambridge: Cambridge University Press, 1973), 8–9.

89. Miller, "Deuteronomy," 4–5.

90. Clements, *Deuteronomy*, 46–47.

91. Otto Eissfeldt, *The Old Testament: An Introduction*, trans. Peter R. Ackroyd (New York: Harper & Row, 1965), 227.

92. William F. Albright, "Some Remarks on the Song of Moses in Deuteronomy XXXII," *Vetus Testamentum* 9 (1959): 346.

93. David A. Robertson, *Linguistic Evidence in Dating Early Hebrew Poetry* (Missoula, Mont.: SBL, for the University of Montana, 1972). The terminus ad quem for this text dates to the post-deuteronomistic period when this piece was supposedly inserted into the Book of Deuteronomy. For this unconvincing argument, see Mayes, "Deuteronomy," 382.

94. Brown et al., *A Hebrew and English Lexicon of the Old Testament*, 849.

95. This story is related in Exod. 17:1–7 and Num. 20:1–11.

96. Cf. Deut. 8:8, 32:13; 2 Kgs. 18:32; 2 Chron. 31:5; Jer. 41:8; Ezek. 16:13, 19; 27:17.

97. Cf. Exod. 3:8, 17; 13:5; 33:3; Lev. 20:24; Num. 13:27; 14:8; 16:13, 14; Deut. 6:3; 11:9; 26:9, 15; 27:3; 31:20; Josh. 5:6; Song of Sol. 4:11; 5:1; Isa. 7:22; Jer. 11:5; 32:22; Ezek. 20:6, 15.

98. The following references in the book of Deuteronomy depict Yahweh as a warrior fighting for Israel: Deut. 6:18–19; 7:1; 9:5; 11:25; 17:20–21, 24; 18:12; 19:1.

99. Driver, *A Critical and Exegetical Commentary on Deuteronomy*, 367.

100. H. A. Hoffner, "Hets," in vol. 5 of *Theological Dictionary of the Old Testament*, ed. G. Johannes Botterweck and Helmer Ringgren, trans. David E. Green (Grand Rapids, Mich.: William B. Eerdsman Publishing Co., 1986), 123.

101. In 2 Sam. 22:15, the arrows/lightning cause *h-m-m*, "confusion." The storm theophanies in Judg. 4:15, Josh. 10:10, and 1 Sam. 7:10 also cause confusion. Significantly, each of these references is evidenced in the corpus of the Deuteronomic History. Furthermore, these references provide conclusive evidence that DTR's hand is active in editing these passages which seem to be associated with Deut. 7:23 which states, "The Lord your God will deliver them [the enemies] up to you, throwing them into utter confusion, until they are wiped out." In Deut. 7:23 and in *all* of these references the same verb *h-m-m* is used.

102. D. Luckenbill, *Ancient Records of Assyria and Babylonia*, 2 vols. (Chicago, 1926–27), 1:record #76.

103. Frank Moore Cross and David Noel Freedman, "The Blessing of Moses," *Journal of Biblical Literature* 67 (1948): 192. William F. Albright dates it to the eleventh century B.C. in his article, "Some Remarks on the Song of Moses in Deuteronomy XXXII," 346.

104. S. R. Driver, *An Introduction to the Literature of the Old Testament* (Cleveland: Meridian Books, 1967), 98.

105. The word Jeshurun is derived from the Hebrew words *yasher*, which means to be upright. It is also used as a nickname for Israel and/or Jacob. This name only occurs four times in the entire Old Testament in Deut. 32:15; 33:5, 26; and Isa. 44:2. For more detailed information, see M. J. Mulder, "Yesurun," in vol. 6 of *Theological Dictionary of the Old Testament*, ed. G. Johannes Botterweck and Helmer Ringgren, trans. David E. Green (Grand Rapids, Mich.: William B. Eerdsman Publishing Co., 1990). The information listed above was taken from pp. 473–75.

106. Patrick D. Miller, *The Divine Warrior in Early Israel* (Cambridge: Harvard University Press, 1973), 105. The Old Testament references that portray Yahweh riding on a chariot through the heavens are 2 Sam. 22:11; Ps. 68:33; Isa. 19:1; and Ezek. 1.

107. Weinfeld, *Deuteronomy and the Deuteronomic School*, 202. The Ugaritic phrase *rkb ʿrpt* is attested in UT, 68:8,29; ʿnt II:40, III:35, IV:48,50; 51:III:11,18, V:122; 76:1,7: III:37; I Aqht 43–44 as noted by Kaiser, "The Ugaritic Pantheon," 268.

108. John Day, "The Old Testament Utilization of Language and Imagery Having Parallels in the Baal Mythology of the Ugaritic Texts" (Ph.D. diss., University of Cambridge, 1973).

109. Norman C. Habel, *Yahweh versus Baal: A Conflict of Religious Cultures* (New York: Bookman Associates, 1964), 81.

CHAPTER 3

WATER
AND STORM POLEMICS
IN JOSHUA AND JUDGES

An examination of the Book of Deuteronomy and the Deuteronomic History has set the stage for a textual analysis of the remaining books of the DH: Joshua through Kings. This corpus of literature, also referred to as the Former Prophets, reflects the Yahwistic hand of DTR throughout. In the Book of Deuteronomy, DTR provides a prophetic prologue to DH; now with the ensuing books we find the prior claims of DTR fulfilled as the entrance and subsequent exilic exit of Israel from her promised land is narrated.

This chapter has two major divisions: the first portion deals with water and storm polemics attested in the Book of Joshua, while the second portion examines this issue as evidenced in the book of Judges.

JOSHUA

DTR concludes the Book of Deuteronomy with the account of the death of Moses and the transfer of leadership to Joshua, the son of Nun (Deut. 34:6,9). The introductory chapter of Joshua echoes this theme by relating Yahweh's call to lead Israel across the Jordan into the promised land (Josh. 1:1–2), confirming that Yahweh will be with Joshua, the servant of Moses, just as he was with Moses (Josh. 1:5). This is reinforced by the water-separation motif, which includes the parting of the Red Sea and the dividing of the Jordan, demonstrating the transferral of Yahweh's divine power.

Joshua 2:9–11

Joshua 2 portrays Joshua sending two spies to Jericho to observe conditions before the Israelite invasion of Canaan (Josh. 2:1). The spies enter the inn of the Canaanite harlot Rahab, who informs them of the psychological condition of her people. Joshua 2:9–11 has the following account:

> (9) And she said unto the men, I know that the Lord has given you the land and that your terror has come upon us, for all the inhabitants of the land are melting because of you. (10) For we have heard how the Lord dried up the water of the Red Sea for you when you came out of Egypt; and what you did unto the two kings of the Amorites, that were on the other side of the Jordan, Sihon and Og, whom you completely destroyed. (11) And when we had heard these things, our hearts melted, and there did not arise again spirit in any man, because of you; for Yahweh is your God, he is God in heaven above and earth beneath.

This text reflects the Canaanites' fear at the dawn of the Israelite conquest of Canaan. DTR's footprints are ever present as the literature reflects the notion that Yahweh has sole control of all creation. "The one thing that does appear to be clear is that the Deuteronomist has introduced his own theological conception with the mouth of Rahab in v. 9–11," observes Butler.[1] On the surface, such theology implies that Yahweh is a divine warrior who has fought and will yet fight Israel's battles. Beneath this explicit claim, however, lies an implicit polemic that requires careful examination.

The inhabitants of the land of Canaan devotedly worshipped Baal Hadad. In the Ugaritic literature we learn of Baal's dominion over Yam (Sea). In the account Kothar-wa-Hasis, the craftsman god, has made for Baal two weapons (named Driver and Chaser), which may possibly symbolize thunder and lightning.[2] In this text Driver is told by Kothar-wa-Hasis the following:

> Drive Sea from his throne, river from the seat of his dominion. You shall swoop in the hands of Baal, like an eagle in his fingers. Strike the head of Prince Sea, between the eyes of Judge River. Let Sea sink and fall to the earth. And the stick swoops in Baal's hands like an eagle in his fingers. It strikes the head of Prince [Sea], between the eyes of Judge River. Sea sinks, falls

> to the earth, his joints fail, his frame collapses. Baal
> pounces and drinks Sea, he destroys Judge River (KTU
> 1.2.IV:19–27).

This pericope from Canaanite literature conveys the idea that Baal rules the sea, while Joshua 2:9–11 appears to convey the implicit message that it is not Baal Hadad, but rather Yahweh, who has power over the sea and is the sole God of heaven and earth. This is characteristic of Deuteronomy.[3] These verses hint that the Canaanites fear Yahweh, because when they hear the dreadful news of his parting of the Red Sea, they realize that it is Yahweh who rules the sea and has power to rule them as well as their god Baal Hadad.

 Joshua 2:9 contains evidence that DTR uses material from the Song of the Sea.[4] DTR portrays Rahab inversely quoting a verse of this Song: she cries in Joshua 2:9a, "Your terror fell upon us"; and in Joshua 2:9b, "All the inhabitants of the land melt away." In comparison, Exodus 15:15b states, "all the inhabitants of Canaan will melt away"; and Exodus 15:16a continues, "Terror will fall upon them."[5]

 The language of Joshua 2:9–11 typifies holy war language, as suggested by the terror that falls upon the Canaanites when they hear of Yahweh's mighty act.[6] Millard C. Lind maintains that such "conventional holy war language when used by Israel must usually be interpreted in the light of Israel's foundational event at the sea."[7] DTR uses the parting of the Red Sea in just this way. Yahweh's victory over the sea may be viewed as the culminating sign of Yahweh's victory over Egypt and her gods. At the same time, DTR seems to relate this story as a sign of Yahweh's imminent conquest of Canaan and Baalism. In this way the story of the Red Sea parting can be seen as a polemic against Israel's gods and enemies on two sides: first, it puts an end to the Egyptian dominion of Israel's past; and second, it affirms that Yahweh has the power to defeat Israel's enemies of the future, particularly the Canaanites, who worship the god of water and storm, Baal Hadad. The Hebrew Bible itself indicates that the ten plagues that fell upon Egypt were a polemic against the Egyptian pantheon. These ten plagues were designed to be a witness "against all the gods of Egypt" (Exod. 12:12) as Yahweh executed his judgments against these false deities (Num. 33:4).

 The background of the Red Sea narrative in Exodus 14–15 suggests that the story was to be viewed more as a polemic against the Canaanite's storm god Baal than as a polemic against the Egyptian deities of Israel's past—though the narrative served a dreadful end to the Egyptian army. It is important to look carefully at this story, because it appears to be the primordial polemical event against Baalism that is related to many subsequent water polemics in the Deuteronomic History.

The first time this narrative occurs, the text twice indicates that the parting of the Red Sea took place at Baal Zephon (Exod. 14:2, 9). Norman Habel explains that "a name such as Baal-Zephon immediately suggests the worship of the Canaanite Baal in this area."[8] In fact, Baal-Zephon (Ugaritic Saphan) was the primary abode of Baal Hadad, as evidenced from the Ugaritic texts.[9] He also regards himself as the "god of Saphan" (god of the north) who dwells in the midst of his mountain.[10]

Noth maintains that these verses (Exod. 14:2, 9) should be identified with the P source.[11] I agree with Noth that these verses show later editing; however, it seems more likely that DTR colored the text in these verses to emphasize that the Red Sea narrative took place at Baal Zephon.

This story seems to have been heightened by DTR because Baalism would have such a devastating impact on the future of Israel, even though evidence suggests that Israel was exposed to Baalism before she left Egypt. Nearly sixty years ago Otto Eissfeldt postulated that a sanctuary was dedicated to Baal Hadad at Baal Zephon.[12] John Gray affirmed Eissfeldt's hypothesis and added, "The most notable cult center of Baal in Egypt was Baal Saphon near Pelusium, E of the Delta." George Beer went so far as to suggest that Israel's deliverance at the Red Sea took place at a Baal sanctuary and was therefore originally attributed to Baal Hadad instead of Yahweh.[13]

Beer may have gone too far. However, in his defense, minimal evidence gleaned from a textual analysis suggests that some of the Hebrew tribes could have conceivably credited Baal for this mighty act, because there was among them a mixed multitude of non-Hebrew people (Exod. 12:38). Moreover, historically it would not make sense to think that when Israel constructed the calf shortly after the Red Sea event (Exod. 32) it was designed as an image of the Apis bull, which was clearly an Egyptian god. Rather, it may have served as a pedestal for either Yahweh or Baal Hadad, as the use of animals and especially the lion and bull as pedestals for deities in the Near East was common.[14] What is most intriguing is that ample evidence portrays the storm god of the Near East riding upon a bull.[15] Furthermore, the text indicates that when Moses saw the calf, he ground it up and forced the Israelites to drink it (Exod. 32:19–20),[16] possibly suggesting that Israel was drinking in the false practices of Baal worship. On the other hand, this act may be viewed as an ordeal whereby the guilty party was cursed.[17]

Other evidence argues that the Hebrew tribes were exposed to Baalism while in Egypt. John Gray thinks that "Baal was one of the Semitic deities whose cult penetrated to Egypt, possibly with the great numbers of Semites deported from Syria and Palestine in the Eighteenth and Nineteenth Dynasties."[18] Claude Schaeffer's excavations of Ras Shamra provide substantial archaeological evidence to demonstrate an active correspondence between Ugarit and Egypt, beginning with the early second millennium and continuing until the fall of Ugarit.[19] Certainly such a correspondence would bring at least a knowledge of Baalism to Egypt.

The idea that Baalism penetrated Egypt is confirmed by Wolfgang Helck's research. Helck provides solid evidence that Baal was associated with the Egyptian god Seth in Egypt.[20] John Van Seters maintains that the iconography of Baal and Seth in Egypt is identical and that Baal is portrayed in the same way in a stele from Ras Shamra.[21] Hermann Kees believes that although the sources we have on the Hyksos period may be scanty, "One thing certain is that the name Seth of Avaris appears for the first time on Egyptian monuments about the time of the Hyksos invasion."[22] Seth, regarded as the god of the storm and desert, was referred to as the "lord of foreign lands."[23] Siegfried Morenz explains that "as the god of foreign parts, he has Anath and Astarte as his companions."[24] This is revealing because we know that Baal's consorts at Ugarit are Anath and Astarte. Helck's evidence also supports the view that the worship of foreign deities was active in Egypt during the period of the Hyksos and that Baal is present there at least one hundred years before the Exodus.

Concerning the connection between the Hyksos, the Israelites in Egypt, and Baal, Frank E. Eakin conjectured that "the Semitic linkage between the Hyksos and the Hebrews would likely lead to a Hebrew awareness of the Baal mythology if this were a part of the Hyksos structure."[25] That this is so may be suggested by the fact that Hyksos scarabs contain the theophoric names of Jacob-Baal[26] and Jacob Hadad[27]; and a foreign king named Jakbaal is evidenced in this period of Hyksos rule.[28] John Bright suggests that these early Hyksos rulers have names that are probably Canaanite or Amorite and that these people worshipped Baal, their chief god, who is also identified with the Egyptian deity Seth.[29]

Whether Baalism was introduced through the instrumentality of the inhabitants of ancient Ugarit or the Hyksos, who would arrive later, is a matter of conjecture. Regardless, what pertains to this study is the notion that the Israelites were exposed to Baalism before their departure from Egypt. This evidence is related to the hypothesis that DTR used implicit water and storm polemics in the DH to demonstrate that Yahweh had proved his point in Egypt: he controlled the domain of Baal (to whom Israel seems to have been exposed and may have worshipped) before Israel ever arrived in the promised land. Furthermore, DTR presents Yahweh as reiterating his claim of power over heaven and earth through repeated demonstrations of water and storm against Israel's enemies; these in turn echo Yahweh's primary pronouncement as Lord of All at the Red Sea. By this argument, DTR presents Yahweh as a never-changing omnipotent God by recounting the victories over the realm of Baal and at the same time leaves Israel without excuse for her flagrant sin of Baal worship.

Joshua 4:23–5:1

The events prior to this text show that Yahweh has magnified Joshua, who leads the children of Israel through the Jordan River on dry ground. This story is set in a covenantal context. When the waters of the Jordan are said to be cut off (Josh. 3:13, 16; 4:7), the verb used is *k-r-t*, meaning "to cut off" or "to make a covenant."[30] Joshua 4:7 strengthens this argument by explaining that "the waters of the Jordan were cut off *because of the ark of the Lord's covenant*" (italics added). It should be noted that this is the only narrative in the entire Hebrew Bible where the Hebrew verb *k-r-t* is used in the water-separation motif. This narrative symbolizes the ritual passing of the Israelites from gentile to covenant soil. Furthermore, the confirmation of this interpretation occurs in Joshua 5:2–3, when Joshua obeys Yahweh's command to circumcise the children of Israel, which immediately follows the cutting off of the waters of the river Jordan.[31]

The text most relevant for our study is Joshua 4:23–5:1. The Israelites have just obeyed Yahweh's instruction to erect twelve stones to commemorate Israel's passing over the Jordan river on dry ground. The text then states:

> (23) For the Lord your God dried up the waters of the
> Jordan before you until you passed, just as the Lord

your God did to the Red Sea, which he dried up before us until we crossed. (24) Thus all the people of the earth will know how mighty is the hand of the Lord, and you shall fear the Lord your God always. (5:1) When the kings of the Amorites on the western side of the Jordan, and all the kings of the Canaanites near the Sea, heard how Yahweh had dried up the waters of the Jordan for the sake of the Israelites until they passed over, their hearts melted, and no spirit was left in them.

Verse 23 ties Yahweh's power over the Red Sea and the Jordan River narratives into one idea. The psalmist did the same when he wrote, "The sea saw and fled, Jordan was turned back" (Ps. 114:3). This same notion occurs in Ugaritic mythology: in the Ugaritic texts, Baal can rend Yam (sea), which includes the idea of controlling the rivers, the extension of the sea.[32] Yam's full name is actually *zbl ym ṯpt nhr*, (Prince Sea, Judge River.)[33] Just as the Red Sea and Jordan River are viewed as one concept, so in Ugaritic literature are Prince Sea and Judge River combined as one idea, as attested in the translation listed above (KTU 1.2.IV:22–28).[34]

In Joshua 4:24 we also see the hand of DTR, which reflects the message in the Rahab narrative in Joshua 2:9–11. In both of these texts, holy war language is used and the idea expressed is that Yahweh is Lord of all. Trent C. Butler views Joshua 4:23–24 as follows:

A temporal clause in 4:23 and a result clause in 4:24...demonstrates the reflection of later generations on the meaning of cultic teaching. The content of the result clause is precisely the teaching of the Deuteronomic school concerning holy war. The teaching is aimed on the surface level to two audiences. First, it seeks to demonstrate to all the enemies of Israel that Israel's God controls the military power to win any battle for Israel and thus is truly Lord of all the earth. Such reaction by the nations should then teach Israel to stand in worshipful awe of her God forever, no matter what happens. The material is not written and given to the nations. It is written and taught only to Israel. Thus the actual purpose of the writer is to bring Israel to reflect upon her history.[35]

Joshua 4:24 promotes the notion that Israel should reflect not only on her history, but on her covenant with Yahweh. Here Israel is instructed to *y-r-ʾ*, (Yahweh)—a Hebrew verbal root most often translated

as "fear" or "reverence."[36] This word is used in the Book of Deuteronomy as well as the DH in a covenantal context. However, "the setting
of this verb within the treaty form in Deuteronomy and dependent texts,
makes it clear that what is meant is neither 'fear' nor 'reverence,' but
something like single-minded and exclusive loyalty."[37] Kamol
Arayaprateep maintains that *y-r-ʾ* in Joshua 4:24 is in fact the key word
in the entire corpus of Joshua 3–5:1 and that this Hebrew word,

> is representative of the typical Deuteronomic conception
> of *y-r-ʾ* which never has anything to do with nations,
> but speaks of Israel in the covenant relationship with
> Yahweh. *y-r-ʾ* (fear) means being faithful to Yahweh,
> i.e., worshipping him alone.[38]

In Joshua 5:1 we again encounter an implicit polemic against
Baalism beneath the surface of the verse. John Gray suggests that this
verse is a Deuteronomic note which reflects the low morale of the
Canaanites and Amorites and emphasizes the miraculous works of
Yahweh.[39] What Gray fails to mention, however, is that the morale
of the Canaanites is directly related to the news of Yahweh's mighty
works. As with Joshua 2:11, when the inhabitants of the land of Canaan
hear how Yahweh has power over water (which is supposedly Baal
Hadad's domain), their hearts melt[40] and they are frightened. With
Rahab's narrative (Josh. 2:9–11), the parting of the Red Sea caused
fright in the Canaanites; in this text (Josh. 4:23–5:1) the parting of the
Jordan also produces fear. Thus these two water-separation stories
constitute water polemics against the Canaanite god Baal Hadad.

Joshua 10:8–11

The final text to consider in the Book of Joshua is Joshua 10:8–11.
Before this text opens, the Israelites are engaged in battle with the
Amorites in the valley of Ajalon. The text reads as follows:

> (8) Yahweh said to Joshua, "Do not fear them for I will
> deliver them into your hands; not one of them will be
> able to withstand you." (9) And Joshua came upon
> them suddenly, marching all night from Gilgal. (10)
> Yahweh confused them before Israel, and smote them
> with a great smiting at Gibeon, and pursued them
> towards the ascent of Beth-horon, and the Lord smote
> them until Azekah and Makkedah. (11) And it came
> to pass in their fleeing before Israel they were descend-
> ing at Bethhorn, Yahweh threw upon them great stones
> from heaven until Azekah, and they died; there were

more who died from the hail stones than who died
because of the sword of the Israelites.

In Joshua 10:8 we again encounter the Hebrew verbal root *y-r-ʾ*,
usually rendered "to fear" or "to reverence." This verse requires not that
Israel fear the enemies of Yahweh, but to "fear" the Lord and to "render"
complete loyalty to Israel's covenant with him. Verse nine indicates
that Joshua came from Gilgal to the place of battle, the place where he
circumcises the men of Israel and where the reproach of Egypt was rolled
away as a renewal of the covenant is made (Josh. 5:8–9). Joshua is
again portrayed as Yahweh's leader in holy war. Like Moses, he is the
instrument through whom Yahweh will work his mighty works.

In verse 10, the word "them" refers to the Amorites, as indicated
by Joshua 10:12. The Amorites are listed with six other groups of
people, inhabitants of Canaan whom Israel is commanded to utterly
destroy in order to prevent the spread of idolatrous worship—which most
often means Baalism (Deut. 7:1–4). The Hebrew verbal root used in
Joshua 10:10 is *h-m-m*, meaning "to confuse" or "to discomfit."[41] As
noted in Chapter 2, this verb is a technical term used in holy war
narratives. In the DH it links this narrative with Judges 4 and 1
Samuel 7, which also portray a setting of holy war. In Deuteronomy
7:23 Yahweh promises his covenant people that he will confuse the
enemies until they are completely destroyed. The use of the verbal root
h-m-m in Deuteronomy 7:23 and here in Joshua 10:10 reveals the hand
of DTR in editing these texts. The words of this passage fulfill those
from the Book of Deuteronomy in the corpus of DH.

Verse 11 in the text specifies that the Amorites are smitten by
great hail stones which Yahweh threw upon them. Exodus 9 indicates
that the Lord did the same to the Egyptians, but the Israelites in the
land of Goshen were not affected (Exod. 9:25–26). Joshua 10:11 conveys
the same idea: the Amorites are smitten with hail stones while the
Israelites go unharmed. In fact, this text leans more towards the
miraculous than the Exodus plague in that the Israelites are pictured
in the land of Goshen when this hail plague fell on the Egyptians in
Egypt. In contrast, in this text (Josh.10: 11) the Amorites and the
Israelites fight side by side, while only the Amorites are smitten.

In Ugaritic literature Baal Hadad also has the ability to send
stones from heaven.

The word of a tree (22)
the whisper of a stone (23)
murmur of heaven with earth (24)

> the deep with the stars (25)
> stones of lightning which heaven does not know (26)
> a matter which people do not know (27)
> and the multitude of the earth do not understand (28)
> I will execute, and I will reveal it in the midst of my
> mountain, the godly Zephon (29) (KTU 1.3 III:22–29).

In line 26, the combined words *abn brq* have created translation problems for scholars. M. D. Cassuto, followed by Marvin Pope, renders the word *ᵓbn* as a construct noun and therefore interprets *ᵓbn brq* to mean "stones of lightning," while Fensham translates these words as "thunder-stones."[42]

To support Pope and Cassuto's translation, it should first be noted that *brq* is normally translated in Hebrew as "lightning."[43] Furthermore, in Exodus 9:23 the polemical hail plague sent upon the Egyptians is accompanied by fire, which seems most logically rendered as lightning. However, Fensham's translation also finds some support in this same verse: *qolot* (noises) are also present, which would best be understood as thunder. Each of these scholars bases their translations on Ezekiel 28:14. In this verse, Cassuto and Pope equate *ᵓabne-esh* with *ᵓbn brq* and translate it as "stones of lightning." Fensham examines these same sets of words and instead chooses the translation "thunder-stones."[44]

Lines 26–27 also demonstrate that the stones that fall from the heavens confuse the people. Perhaps these "stones of lightning" can be viewed literally as a great hail storm. This corroborates Joshua 10:10–12, wherein similar confusion is due to the large hail stones of a hail storm.[45] Finally, another possible corollary is that Baal sends these stones upon his sacred soil of Mount Zephon, just as Yahweh hurls great stones on his sacred covenant land to demonstrate his power, which is what seems to be implied in regard to Baal in this Ugaritic text.

What is important here is not so much the exact translation of *abn brq* but rather the often overlooked interpretation. In this Ugaritic mythological text, Baal is portrayed with power to send stones from heaven; therefore, he is recognized as the Lord of the storm with the inherent ability to send hail stones.

Joshua 10:10–11 describes a terrible hail storm, wherein DTR has apparently portrayed Yahweh as a God who acts not as Baal in a mendacious mythology, but rather as a divine warrior who acts in history.[46] Yahweh demonstrates his power through storms that include great hail stones, the very instruments that Baal is said to control—in the destruction of Baal's followers. In this way Yahweh asserts his claims that he is, as always, Lord of heaven and earth, superior to Baal.

Frank Eakin argues emphatically that, "no passage in the Book of Joshua...can be interpreted legitimately as an explicit conflict between Yahwism and Baalism."[47] Although this may be true, Eakin fails to consider evidence that suggests an implicit conflict against Baalism through water and storm polemics. The analysis of these texts in the Book of Joshua surely strengthens this claim.

JUDGES

All three polemical texts analyzed in this study of the Book of Joshua are part of the division of that book known as the conquest of Canaan. This division (Josh. 1–12) portrays Israel's entrance into the land of Canaan as a holy war that ended in the sudden and total victory of Israel over all the inhabitants of Canaan.[48] However, as John Bright explains, "the Bible presents another picture of the occupation of Palestine that makes it clear that it was a long process, accomplished by the efforts of individual clans, and but partially completed. This is best seen in Judg., ch. 1."[49]

Judges 1 provides information on the Canaanite remnants in the land following the conquest account in Joshua 1–12. It also serves as a transition to explain why Israel did not achieve a complete victory over the Canaanites. According to Eakin, Judges 2:6–3:6 presents a biased explanation by the Deuteronomic historians of what was the root of this issue.[50] "This text has abundant terms and expressions typical of the Dtr history," remarked J. Alberto Soggin.[51]

The text begins with Joshua concluding his final speech in which he dismisses the people to enter into their lands of inheritance (Judg. 2:6). It further indicates that all Israel was righteous during Joshua's lifetime, but when he died, a new generation arose that did not know the mighty works of the Lord (Judg. 2:7–10). Instead, as Judges 2:11–13 states, they turned to Baalism:

> (11) And the Israelites did what was evil in the eyes of Yahweh. They worshipped the Baalim.[52] (12) And they forsook the Lord God of their fathers, who had brought them out of the land of Egypt. They followed other gods from among the gods of the peoples around them, and bowed down to them; they provoked the Lord. (13) They forsook Yahweh and worshipped Baal and the Ashtaroth.[53]

DTR then adds that Yahweh was angered because Israel had transgressed the covenant; he declared that he would no longer do his part in driving the remaining Canaanites hastily out of the land, but would leave them in order to see whether Israel would be obedient to him (Judg. 2:20–23). The remaining portion of the text (Judg. 3:1–6) lists the groups of people left in the land to prove Israel and adds that the Israelites intermarried with the Canaanites and worshipped their gods. The verse that follows (Judg. 3:7) states that Israel was again involved with Baalism. Judges 3–4 then proceed to describe the cycle of apostasy inherent not only in the remainder of this chapter, but throughout the whole book of Judges.

Judges 5

The Song of Deborah is considered one of the earliest texts in the Hebrew Bible. Scholars consistently date it to the end of the twelfth century B.C.[54] Millard C. Lind writes that "the Song of Deborah (Judg. 5) is one of the two substantial poems in the Bible probably composed in the twelfth century B.C. The other is the Song of the Sea.... The Song of Deborah, like the Song of the Sea, is a unified victory hymn."[55] Alexander Globe adds that the Song of Deborah has the appearance of a literary unit.[56] Deuteronomic revision is silent; rather DTR seems to have included this story as a whole in the DH for a didactic purpose. The text may be viewed as a sign that the conquest of the Canaanites and their kings has come to a temporary end.[57]

J. Alberto Soggin summarizes the contents of the Song of Deborah:

> The theme of the ancient song is how Israel, in the course of a battle, succeeded in vanquishing a coalition of Canaanite city states situated around the plain of Jezreel and here assembled under the leadership of a certain Sisera. This is one of the regions which according to Judg. 1 Israel did not succeed in occupying because it was tenaciously and skillfully defended by its inhabitants.[58]

The possible polemical elements first occur in Judges 5:4–5:

> (4) Yahweh, when you went out from Seir, when you marched from the field of Edom, the earth trembled and the heavens dropped, the clouds also dropped water. (5) The mountains flowed from before the Lord, the One of Sinai,[59] the Lord God of Israel.

The idea that Yahweh comes from the south out of his ancient abode in Sinai is strengthened by a comparative verse found in the Blessing of Moses: "Yahweh came from Sinai, and beamed forth unto them from Seir" (Deut. 33:2).[60] C. F. Burney adds, "Here Sinai is grouped with Se'ir, i.e., the mountain range of Edom which runs north and south from the Dead Sea to the Gulf of 'Akaba."[61]

Yahweh's march from his seat on Sinai in the south, endowed with the power of storm, contrasts polemically with the homeland of Baal Hadad. Baal is said to reside on Mount Saphon in the north, a comparison that may be viewed as the direct antithesis to the abode of Yahweh.[62] Furthermore, that Sinai is such a dry, desolate region as compared to the fertile area of Mount Saphon emphasizes the notion that Yahweh is able to provide moisture in any location.

Verse 4 indicates that when Yahweh left his abode, the earth trembled and the heavens dropped water. This trembling seems to be connected to thunder and lightning, which are commonly associated with Yahweh's theophany on Mount Sinai (Exod. 19:16). When Baal Hadad makes his seasonal advent, there is also a similar theophany. One Ugaritic text states, "The time for his rain Baal is appointing, the time for moisture and the utterance of his voice in the clouds, for the release of lightning-flashes to the earth" (KTU 1.4.V:6–9).[63]

The Song of Deborah contains additional storm polemics against Baalism. The text ultimately attributes the Israelite victory over the Canaanites to Yahweh: "(20) They fought from heaven, the stars in their courses fought against Sisera. (21) The torrent Kishon swept them away, that ancient torrent, the torrent Kishon" (Judg. 5:20–21).

Verse 20 points out that the stars fought against Sisera—an interesting comment when it is understood that the stars are the source of rain in the Ugaritic myth (KTU 1.3.II:41). This strengthens the argument that this is a rainstorm.[64] Furthermore, in verse 21, the torrent Kishon is mentioned twice, which advances the idea that this is indeed a mighty storm.[65]

The prose account[66] of the victory indicates that Yahweh threw Sisera and his chariots and all his army into a panic[67] (Judg. 4:15), confirmation that this is a divine conflict. Yairah Amit believes "that type of war, which is uncharacterizable in human terms, is viewed as a sign of or convention for a divine war in which man's share in the determination of the outcome is secondary."[68] No doubt this story portrays a terrible storm that immobilized the Canaanite chariots for the flooding water mired their wheels in the mud.[69] Josephus writes, "So the battle began; and when they were come to close fight, there came down from heaven a great storm with a vast quantity of rain and hail" (Antiq. V.5.4).[70] Judges 4:15–16 also indicates that Baraq fought the Canaanites with the edge of the sword and pursued them. Perhaps Baraq symbolizes Yahweh's weapon of storm, since the Hebrew word *baraq* means "lightning" or "lightning flash."[71] Just as Baraq pursued the Canaanites with the sword, so Yahweh figuratively pursued the Canaanite worshippers of Baal with his sword of lightning. In this way Baraq's battle against the Canaanites epitomizes Yahweh's divine war with the Canaanite storm god.

Judges 6

Following the Song of Deborah (Judg. 5) are the Gideon narratives comprising Judges 6–8. The sources used in the Gideon stories and their compositional dates have been disputed among scholars.[72] However, there is some general scholarly agreement that the first chapter (Judg. 6), which deals with the call and mission of Gideon, contains polemical elements against Baalism. The composition of the chapter is outlined as follows:[73]

> 6:1–10—The oppression of the Midianites.
> 6:11–24—The first account of Gideon's call at the altar of Ophrah.
> 6:25–32—The second account of Gideon's call, the destruction of the altar.
> 6:33–35—Israel called to gather to fight children of the east.
> 6:36–40—The tests involving fleece and dew.

According to C. F. Burney, verses 7–10 of the first part of the text (6:1–10) contain polemical material against Baalism that is characteristic of the style of the later E stratum.[74] However, J. Alberto Soggin counters that these verses along with the entire segment (6:1–10) were composed by DTR.[75] The best evidence for sustaining Soggin's hypothesis is the last verse in the segment: "And I said to you, I am Yahweh your God, don't fear the gods of the Amorites in whose land you dwell; but you did not obey my voice" (Judg. 6:10). Again, in typical Deuteronomic fashion, Israel is told not to fear other gods.

Scholars generally consider the second part (6:11–24) to be J material;[76] it represents a direct call to Gideon by Yahweh's messenger to deliver Israel from the Midianites. The third part of the chapter

(6:25–32) is generally ascribed to the E stratum,[77] although there is also present a Deuteronomic redaction. This important portion of text reveals the explicit polemics against Baalism inherent in this chapter and also sets the stage for the implicit polemic against Baal that follows in Judges 6:36–40.

In this pericope Yahweh tells Gideon (whose name means *hacker* or *hewer*)[78] to "pull down the altar of Baal, that belongs to your father, and cut down the sacred post which is beside it" (Judg. 6:25–26). Here, we can detect the hand of DTR because these verses serve as a fulfillment of Deuteronomy 7:5, "you shall pull down their altars...cut down their sacred posts." Gideon obeys this command, and as a result the people of Ophrah seek his life for destroying their Baalist sanctuary (Judg. 6:26–30). Gideon's father, Joash, then tries to vindicate his son by proposing that if Baal really is a god "let him plead for himself" (Judg. 6:31). The text then states "That day they named him Jerubbaal, meaning 'let Baal plead with him' because he [Gideon] tore down his altar" (Judg. 6:32).[79]

This literary evidence shows not only that the writer wants it known that syncretism is present but also that there is express conflict between Yahwism and Baalism. According to Bernard W. Anderson, "this story is important because it shows how deeply Canaanite rites and conceptions had infiltrated, and because it shows how Israel's strength in time of crisis was connected with a revival of a vigorous faith in Yahweh."[80]

This pericope (Judg. 6:25–32) does indeed denote an explicit conflict with Baalism, and at the same time clarifies the less apparent moisture polemic against Baal found in the text of Judges 6:36–40:

> (36) And Gideon said to God, If you really expect to deliver Israel by my hand, as you have said, (37) Behold, I will set a fleece of wool on the threshing floor; and if dew falls only on the fleece and all the ground stays dry, I will know that you will deliver Israel through me, as you said you would. (38) And it was so; for he rose up early the next day and he squeezed the fleece and wrung out the dew out of the fleece, a bowlful of water. (39) Then Gideon said to God, Do not be angry with me if I speak just once more. Please let me prove only this once with the fleece; let it now be dry only upon the fleece, and upon all the ground let there be dew. 40. And God did so that night; for it was dry upon the fleece only, and there was dew

on all of the ground.

In verse 36 Gideon is viewed as the person designated to deliver Israel from the Midianites and their Canaanite allies (Judg. 6:14, 16, 33). The Hebrew Bible indicates that before the period of the Israelite settlement in Canaan, the Midianites had led Israel into Baalistic practices when Israel was joined to Baal-Peor, while dwelling at Shittim (Num.25:1–7). Verses 37–38 relate the first experiment with dew. According to S. Tolkowsky, this was not a miracle because it was done in accordance with nature's physical laws: "the fleece, composed of long thin hair, attracts such a large quantity of moisture which is not again evaporated because the leather of the fleece itself and the lower part of the wool keep the condensed dew insulated and protected from the warmth of the soil."[81] However, Tolkowsky does acknowledge that the reversal of this experiment discussed in Judges 6:39–40 "is in direct conflict with the same natural laws."[82]

Soggin suggests that this second experiment is a miraculous sign and attributes it to DTR.[83] The sign again demonstrates Yahweh's divine ability to control the elements of nature. Dew is considered a precious commodity in the Hebrew Bible and a gift from heaven in the Deuteronomic corpus (Deut. 33:13).[84]

It is important to note that the text portrays Gideon specifically requesting this dew experiment. When analyzed with the understanding that he has just overthrown the altar of Baal, it takes on added significance. The text seems to indicate that Gideon wants to ensure that Yahweh will be with him and his people since he has destroyed his hometown's altar of Baal. Furthermore, when this knowledge is coupled with the perception that the enemies he faces worship Baal, the polemic is made manifest. The best evidence for an implicit Baal polemic, however, comes from an understanding that Baal controls the dew.

A tablet excavated in 1961 describes Baal on the top of Mount Zephon encompassed by lightning and with dew streaming from him.[85] An Ugaritic text (KTU 1.19.I:42–46) states the following:

> Seven years shall Baal fail,
> Eight the rider of clouds.
> There shall be no dew, no rain
> No surging of the deeps,
> Neither the goodness of Baal's voice.

The Ugaritic materials also show that one of Baal's three daughters is called *Tly*. Walter C. Kaiser explains the background of this goddess:

> This goddess is called the "girl of rain," *bt.rb*. The root of *rb* must be *rbb* reflecting Hebrew rabib, "rain," "shower" since it is used in parallelism to *tl*, "dew" in texts like 'nt:II:39; I Aqht.44, 2003:1. This daughter is the goddess of the morning dew and thereby reflects Baal's interest not only in the rainy season, but in the year round aspects of fertility.[86]

Tly, and her sisters, represent different aspects of fertility over which Baal is said to have dominion. "They have no independence in the myth, but by virtue of their relationship to the rain god [Baal] are completely dependent on him," explains Lawrence E. Toombs.[87]

This combined evidence suggests that DTR portrays Gideon as a man who wants direct affirmation that Yahweh is with him. The literature suggests that this issue is heightened by the understanding that Gideon has overthrown Baal who reportedly controls the dew. Therefore, the fact that Gideon requests the miraculous sign of Yahweh's dominion over dew suggests that this is an implicit water polemic against the storm god Baal.

The evidence in this chapter demonstrates how through implicit Baalistic polemics, Yahweh is uniquely Lord of all aspects of storm and water, including hail, thunder, lightning, seas, rivers, and dew.

NOTES

1. Trent C. Butler, *Joshua*, vol. 7 of *Word Biblical Commentary*, ed. David A. Hubbard and Glenn W. Barker (Waco, Texas: Word Books, 1982), 31.

2. For more information concerning Kothar-wa-Hasis, see Oldenburg, *The Conflict between El and Ba'al in Canaanite Religion*, 95–100; Kaiser, "The Ugaritic Pantheon," 122–25.

3. See, for example, Deut. 4:39.

4. The story of the parting of the Red Sea has its earliest written attestation in the Song of the Sea, also known as the Song of Miriam (Exod. 15). Frank Moore Cross and David Noel Freedman, "The Song of Miriam," *Journal of Near Eastern Studies* 13 (January-October 1955): 239.

5. Millard C. Lind, *Yahweh is a Warrior: The Theology of Warfare in Ancient Israel* (Scottdale, Penn.: Herald Press, 1973), 80.

6. For an excellent treatise on the holy war language used in Josh. 2:9–11, see Dennis J. McCarthy, "Some Holy War Vocabulary In Joshua 2," *Catholic Biblical Quarterly* 33 (April 1971): 228–30.

7. Lind, *Yahweh is a Warrior*, 75.

8. Habel, *Yahweh versus Baal*, 20–21.

9. KTU 1.4.IV:19.

10. KTU 1.3.III:29.

11. Martin Noth, *A History of Pentateuchal Traditions*, trans. with an intro. by Bernard W. Anderson (Chico, Calif.: Scholars Press, 1981), 269.

12. See Otto Eissfeldt, *Baal Zephon, Zeus Kasios und der Durchzug der Israeliten durchs Meer* (Halle: Max Niemeyer Verlag, 1932).

13. John Gray, "Baal (Deity)," in vol. 1 of *The Interpreter's Dictionary of the Bible*, ed. George A. Buttrick, Thomas Samuel Kepler, John Knox,

Herbert Gordon May, Samuel Terrein, and Emory Stevens Bucker (Nashville: Abingdon Press, 1982), 328–29. George Beer, *Exodus*, vol. 3 of *Handbuch zum Alten Testament*, ed. Otto Eissfeldt (Tubingen: J. C. B. Mohr, 1939), 75.

14. James B. Pritchard, *The Ancient Near East in Pictures Relating to the Old Testament* (Princeton, N.J.: Princeton University Press, 1954). See picture numbers 470–74; 479, 486, 522, 525, 526, 531, 534, 537, 830, 835.

15. Ibid., picture numbers 500, 501, 531.

16. This story is also related in Deut. 9:21. However, in this text the ground calf is thrown upon the water that comes from the mountain. Although the text does not state that Moses made the children of Israel drink it, the implication is that they did.

17. For a treatise of the water ordeal, see Num. 5:11–31.

18. Gray, "Baal (Deity)," 328–29.

19. Schaeffer, *The Cuneiform Texts of Ras Shamra-Ugarit*, 9ff.

20. Wolfgang Helck, *Die Beziehungen Ägyptens zu Vorderasien im 3. und 2. Jahrtausend V. Chr.*, band 5, *Agyptologisch Abhandlungen*, herausgeben von Wolfgang Helck und Eberhard Otto (Wiesbaden: Otto Harrassowitz, 1971), 447–50.

21. John Van Seters, *The Hyksos: A New Investigation* (New Haven, Conn.: Yale University Press, 1966), 174–75.

22. Hermann Kees, *Ancient Egypt: A Cultural Topography* (Chicago: University of Chicago Press, 1961), 197.

23. Siegfried Morenz, *Egyptian Religion*, trans. Ann E. Keep (Ithaca, N.Y.: Cornell University Press, 1973), 268.

24. Ibid., 269.

25. Frank E. Eakin, Jr., "The Reed Sea and Baalism," *Journal of Biblical Literature* 86, pt. 4 (December 1967): 381–82.

26. S. Yeivin, "Ya'qob'el," *The Journal of Egyptian Archaeology* 45 (1959): 16–18.

27. Thomas L. Thompson, *The Historicity of the Patriarchal Narratives: The Quest for the Historical Abraham* (New York: Walter de Gruyter, 1974), 42–51. This article discusses the Hyksos scarab names of Jacob Hadad as well as Jacob Baal.

28. B. G. Trigger, B. J. Kemp, D. O'Connor, and A. B. Llody, *Ancient Egypt: A Social History* (New York: Cambridge University Press, 1983), 158.

29. John Bright, *A History of Israel*, 3d ed. (Philadelphia: Westminster Press, 1981), 60.

30. Brown et al., *A Hebrew and English Lexicon of the Old Testament*, 503–4. There is also attested here many references to *k-r-t* used in the sense of cutting or making a covenant.

31. The fact that circumcision is performed is an obvious key that the Abrahamic covenant is being renewed. See Gen. 17:7–12.

32. Gaster, *Thespis*, 123.

33. Kaiser, "The Ugaritic Pantheon," 108. It should be noted that the name Tapit Nahar may also be viewed as an epithet for Yam; however, I choose to follow Kaiser's choice and refer to these as part of the full name of Yam.

34. William F. Albright, "Zabul Yamm and Thapit-Nahar in the Combat between Baal and the Sea," *Journal of the Palestine Oriental Society* 16 (1936): 20, states: "Just why the 'judge river' and the 'exalted one, Sea' were equated is more difficult to determine, but one may suspect that the Syrian personification of rivers in the form of dragons is ultimately responsible. It would be very easy to combine two water-monsters with similar characteristics."

35. Butler, *Joshua*, 51.

36. For an exhaustive list for the translation of *y-r-ɔ* as "fear" or "reverence," see Brown et al., *A Hebrew and English Lexicon of the Old Testament*, 431.

37. Robert G. Boling, *Joshua: A New Translation with Notes and Commentary*, vol. 6 of *The Anchor Bible*, ed. W. F. Albright and D. N. Freedman (Garden City, N.Y.: Doubleday, 1982), 187.

38. Kamol Arayaprateep, "A Note on yr' in Jos. IV 24," *Vetus Testamentum* 22 (April 1972): 241.

39. John Gray, ed., "Joshua, Judges and Ruth," in *The Century Bible*, new. ed. (London: Nelson, 1967), 68.

40. Brown et al., *A Hebrew and English Lexicon of the Old Testament*, 587–88, defines the Hebrew verbal root *m-s-s* as "to dissolve" or "to melt." Dr. Harris Lenowitz pointed out to me that the usage of this word may suggest that the hearts of the Canaanites liquify and become subject to Yahweh's control.

41. Brown et al., *A Hebrew and English Lexicon of the Old Testament*, 243.

42. M. D. Cassuto, *From Adam to Noah*, 2d ed. (N.p., 1953), 50–51; Pope, "El in the Ugaritic Texts," 99–100; F. C. Fensham, "Thunder–stones in Ugarit," *Journal of Near Eastern Studies* 18 (1959): 273–74.

43. Brown et al., *A Hebrew and English Lexicon of the Old Testament*, 140.

44. Ibid. Fensham maintains that these thunder-stones are in reality firestones or flint. He seems to have misunderstood the context of Ezek. 28:14 wherein he finds that in the verse before (Exod 28:13) the text is referring to precious stones. Therefore, I would understand *ᵓbne-esh* in this particular context to mean something like stones of splendor or precious stones.

45. C. F. Keil and F. Delitzsch, *Joshua, Judges and Ruth*, vol. 4 of *Biblical Commentary on the Old Testament*, trans. James Martin (Grand Rapids, Mich.: William B. Eerdsman Publishing Co., 1950), 106; and Boling, *Joshua: A New Translation with Notes and Commentary*, 282, also interpret this text as evidence of hail stones in a great hail storm.

46. For a thorough discussion of Yahweh as a divine warrior, see Miller, *The Divine Warrior in Early Israel*; Lind, *Yahweh Is a Warrior*; Cross, *Canaanite Myth and Hebrew Epic*, 91–194.

47. Eakin, "The Relationship between Yahwism and Baalism During the Pre–Exilic Period."

48. Bright, *A History of Israel*, 129.

49. Ibid.

50. Eakin, "The Relationship between Yahwism and Baalism During the Pre-Exilic Period," 93–94.

51. J. Alberto Soggin, *Judges: A Commentary*, 2d ed., trans. John Bowden (London: SCM Press, 1987), 40. For a detailed discussion of the Deuteronomistic editing in the book of Judges as a whole, see Mayes, *The Story of Israel Between Settlement and Exile*; W. L. Moran, "A Study of the Deuteronomistic History," *Biblica* 46 (1965): 222–28; Polzin, *Moses and the Deuteronomist*, 146–204.

52. Walter Gerhardt, Jr., "The Weather-God in the Ancient Near Eastern Literature with Special Reference to Hebrew Bible" (Ph.D. diss., The Dropsie College for Hebrew and Cognate Learning, 1963), 228, states: "I take Ba'alim to be of the same religious structure as elohim, i.e., not Ba'als, but Ba'al who was represented in many areas through local shrines, but had unity of person and power even though he was represented in a multiple of locales." Soggin, *Judges*, 43, indicates that he believes that Baal in the plural form is characteristic of the book of Deuteronomy and the DH and agrees with Gerhardt that Baalim represents various manifestations of the same god, Baal. For an excellent treatise on the meaning of Baalim, see Otto Eissfeldt, "Ba'alsamen und Jahwe," *Zeitschrift für die alttestamentliche Wissenschaft* 57 (1939): 1–31.

53. Robert G. Boling, *Judges*, vol. 6A of *The Anchor Bible*, ed. W. F. Albright and D. N. Freedman (Garden City, N.Y.: Doubleday, 1964), 74, maintains that the word Ashtaroth should be understood as the consort of Baal designated Asherah (Judg. 3:7) or Astarte (Judg. 10:6). He further states that the plural form of her name is "not to be taken numerically as she is one who in herself sums up the variations of her identity in numerous forms and places."

54. Robertson, *Linguistic Evidence in Dating Early Hebrew Poetry*, 155; Miller, *The Divine Warrior in Early Israel*, 87; Lind, *Yahweh Is a*

Warrior, 66. On the basis of archaeological evidence, William F. Albright, "The Song of Deborah in the Light of Archaeology," *BASOR* 62 (April 1936): 29, dates the Song of Deborah to 1125 B.C., which has proved to be in harmony with these modern scholars listed above who come to conclusions based on literary evidence.

55. Lind, *Yahweh Is a Warrior*, 66. For an excellent discussion regarding the relationship between the Song of the Sea (Exod. 15) and the Song of Deborah (Judg. 5), see David Noel Freedman, "Early Israelite History in the Light of the Early Israelite Poetry," in *Unity and Diversity: Essays in the History, Literature and Religion of the Ancient Near East*, ed. H. Goedicke and J. J. M. Roberts (Baltimore: Johns Hopkins University Press, 1975), 3–35.

56. Alexander Globe, "The Literary Structure and Unity of the Song of Deborah," *Journal of Biblical Literature* 93 (December 1974): 511.

57. David Noel Freedman, "Who Is Like Thee Among The Gods," in *Ancient Israelite Religion: Essays in Honor of Frank Moore Cross*, ed. Patrick D. Miller, Jr., Paul D. Hanson, and S. Dean McBride (Philadelphia: Fortress Press, 1987), 334.

58. J. Alberto Soggin, *Introduction to the Old Testament: From Its Origin To The Closing Of The Alexandrian Canon*, 3d ed. (Louisville, Ky: Westminster/John Knox Press, 1989), 202.

59. Albright, "The Song of Deborah in the Light of Archaeology," 30, states: "In v. 5 we find the phrase ze Sinai, which is commonly translated 'this is Sinai,'...and is considered as a gloss to 'mountains'.... Now we know that in North Canaanite, just as in later North Arabic, appellation of deity were sometimes formed with the demonstrative pronoun d.... There can be little doubt that ze Sinai is an archaic appellation of Yahweh, 'the One of Sinai.'"

60. See also Hab. 3:3, which indicates that Yahweh came from the south.

61. C. F. Burney, *The Book of Judges with an Introduction and Notes on the Hebrew Text of the Book of Kings with an Introduction and Appendix* (New York: KTAV Publishing House, 1970), 109.

62. Habel, *Yahweh versus Baal*, 13–14.

63. John Gray, "Israel in the Song of Deborah," in *Ascribe to the Lord: Biblical and Other Studies in Memory of Peter C. Craigie*, ed. Lyle Eslinger and Glen Taylor (Sheffield: JSOT Press, 1988), 425–26.

64. Various scholars follow this line of thinking. See, for example, Gray, "Joshua, Judges and Ruth," 289; J. Blenkinsopp, "Ballad Style and Psalm Style in the Song of Deborah," *Biblica* 42 (1961): 73; Globe, "The Literary Structure and Unity of the Song of Deborah," 501. Against this interpretation, see John F. A. Sawyer, "From Heaven Fought the Stars, (Judges V 20)," *Vetus Testamentum* 31 (1981): 88, who maintains that Judg. 5:20 is associated with Josh. 10:10–12 in that the writer of the Judg. 5:20 account was affected by the eclipse discussed in Josh. 10:10–12 and therefore wrote about stars.

65. Lind, *Yahweh Is a Warrior*, 70.

66. Simon J. De Vries, "Temporal Terms As Structural Elements in the Holy War Tradition," *Vetus Testamentum* 25 (January 1975): 84 maintains that this chapter is very old and contains material from ancient traditions. Lind, *Yahweh Is a Warrior*, 74 dates this prose text to the tenth century. For a detailed analysis of the differences between the prose narrative (Judg. 4) and the poetic victory song (Judg. 5), see George Foot Moore, *A Critical and Exegetical Commentary on Judges*, vol. 7 of *The International Critical Commentary*, ed. S. R. Driver, Alfred Plummer, and Charles A. Briggs (New York: Charles Scribner's Sons, 1895), 107ff.

67. This Hebrew verbal root *h-m-m* again appears and suggests that perhaps this is a Deuteronomistic redaction.

68. Yairah Amit, "Judges 4: Its Contents and Forms," *Journal for the Study of the Old Testament* 39 (1987): 95.

69. H. H. Rowley, "Israel, History of (Israelites)," in vol. 2 of *The Interpreter's Dictionary of the Bible*, ed. George A. Buttrick, Thomas Samuel Kepler, John Knox, Herbert Gordon May, Samuel Terrein, and Emory Stevens Bucker (Nashville: Abingdon Press, 1982), 754.

70. This statement is taken from William Whiston's translation of *Josephus Complete Works* (Grand Rapids, Mich.: Kregel Publications, 1978), 115. This interpretation is also maintained by other scholars.

For example, see Peter C. Craigie, "Some Further Notes on the Song of Deborah," *Vetus Testamentum* 22 (July 1972): 352.

71. Brown et al., *A Hebrew and Lexicon of the Old Testament*, 140.

72. Jeremiah Unterman, "Gideon," in *Harper's Bible Dictionary*, ed. Paul J. Achtemeier, Roger S. Borass, Michael Fishbane, Pheme Perkins, and William O. Walker, Jr. (San Francisco: Harper & Row, 1985), 346.

73. This outline is an adaptation from Soggin, *Judges*, 108–9.

74. Burney, *The Book of Judges*, 177.

75. Soggin, *Judges*, 108.

76. Moore, *A Critical Exegetical Commentary on Judges*, 182. The identification of this strata as J is also followed by Burney, *The Book of Judges*, 177.

77. Moore, *A Critical Exegetical Commentary on Judges*, 191, 198; Burney, *The Book of Judges*, 178.

78. Albright, *Yahweh and the Gods of Canaan*, 199 n. 101.

79. For a detailed discussion of the names and association between Gideon and Jerubbaal, see J. A. Emerton, "Gideon and Jerubbaal," *The Journal of Theological Studies* 27, pt. 2 (1976): 289–312.

80. Bernard W. Anderson, *Understanding the Old Testament*, 3d ed. (Englewood Cliffs, N.J.: Prentice-Hall, 1975), 153–54.

81. S. Tolkowsky, "Gideon's Fleece," *Journal of the Palestine Oriental Society* 3 (1923): 198. This reasoning is also followed by Gray, "Joshua, Judges and Ruth," 302; and Boling, *Judges*, 141.

82. Ibid.

83. Soggin, *Judges*, 133–34.

84. See also Gen. 27:28.

85. Andre Caquot and Maurice Sznycer, *Ugaritic Religion* (Leiden: E. J. Brill, 1980), 13.

86. Kaiser, "The Ugaritic Pantheon," 103.

87. Toombs, "Baal, Lord of the Earth: The Ugaritic Epic," 620–21.

CHAPTER 4

WATER
AND STORM POLEMICS
IN THE BOOKS OF SAMUEL

A question which continues to trouble modern scholars is how much DTR compiled or composed in this stratum of the DH.[1] Martin Noth, who first proposed the idea of DTR in the DH, argues that "Deuteronomic editing of the books of Samuel is somewhat limited. Here the Deuteronomic writer was able to take over the extensive collections of traditions, compiled long before his time."[2] John Van Seters counters, stating that "Noth's recovery of this author is commendable, but Noth did not go far enough. He still attributed too little of the work to the author himself and too much to his sources and traditions."[3] In the polemical material under consideration for this study, we see a combination of both original and traditional materials.

1 SAMUEL 7:3–12

The first polemical pericope to be discussed is 1 Samuel 7:3–12:

(3) And Samuel spoke to all the house of Israel saying, "If you intend to turn to Yahweh with all your heart, then you must put away the foreign gods and the Ashtaroth and prepare your hearts to the Lord and serve/worship him alone, and he will deliver you out of the hands of the Philistines." (4) Then the children of Israel removed the Baalim and the Ashtaroth, and served/worshipped only Yahweh. 5. And Samuel said, "Gather all Israel to Mizpah and I will pray in your behalf to the Lord." (6) And they assembled at Mizpah, and they drew water and poured it out before Yahweh, and they fasted on that day and said there, "We have

sinned against the Lord," and Samuel judged the
children of Israel at Mizpah. (7) And when the
Philistines heard that the children of Israel had
gathered to Mizpah, the lords of the Philistines went
up against Israel. And when the children of Israel
heard, they feared the Philistines. (8) And the children
of Israel said to Samuel, "Don't be silent in crying to
Yahweh our God for us, that he will save us from the
hand of the Philistines." (9) And Samuel took a sucking
lamb and sacrificed it as a whole burnt offering to
Yahweh; and Samuel cried to the Lord for Israel, and
Yahweh answered him. (10) For as Samuel was
offering up the burnt offering, the Philistines drew near
to fight against Israel, but Yahweh thundered with a
great sound/voice on that day upon the Philistines and
discomfited them, and they were smitten before Israel.
(11) And the men of Israel went out of Mizpah and
pursued the Philistines and smote them until they
came under Beth-car. (12) Then Samuel took a stone
and erected it between Mizpah and Shen, and named
it Eben-ezer, and said, "Until now, Yahweh has helped
us."

Henry Preserved Smith was one of the first scholars to argue that
this story reflects the style of Deuteronomic editing that is found in the
Book of Judges. Israel is in bondage due to idolatrous worship, yet
miraculously delivered when she returns to Yahweh.[4] He suggests that
the word *serve* in verse 3 should be understood in the sense of
worshipping Yahweh and reflects Deuteronomic editing.[5] Robert Polzin
agrees, adding that the addition of the word *levaddo*, (alone) echoes
DTR's ideal perspective of serving only Yahweh and none other.[6]

We again encounter in verse 3 the covenantal condition of blessings
that come as a result of obedience. Israel is to worship only Yahweh;
she is instructed in verse 3, "to return unto Yahweh, with all your
heart." According to Hans Walter Wolff, this summons to return to
Yahweh represents the true kerygma of the entire Deuteronomic
History.[7] P. Kyle McCarter maintains that this phrase is a Deuteronomic cliche, well established in Book of Deuteronomy as well as the
DH as a whole.[8] McCarter further suggests of verses 3–4 that there
is Deuteronomic interpolation which is probably founded on Judges 10:6–
16, in Israel's crying out to Yahweh, "we have forsaken our God, and
also served/worshipped Baalim" (Judg. 10:10). McCarter explains:

> The purpose of the present interpolation, therefore, is
> to incorporate the story of Samuel into the Deutero-
> nomistic theology of history as it is present in the book
> of Judges, where the premonarchial experience of Israel
> is related according to a rigid, fourfold pattern of
> apostasy, punishment, repentance and deliverance.[9]

A.D.H. Mayes agrees with McCarter and provides further evidence
to strengthen the claim that the hand of DTR is apparent in these verses
and those that follow, in stating that,

> there is a clear connection between 7.3ff. and what has
> been seen to be deuteronomistic passages in Judges
> (Judg. 2:11ff.; 3:7ff.; 10:6ff.)—the reference to Israel as
> serving the Baals and the Ashtaroth, crying to Yahweh,
> the presentation of Samuel as deliverer and judge, the
> acknowledgment 'we have sinned' (I Sam. 7:6; Judg.
> 10:10).[10]

In 1 Samuel 7:3–4 the Deuteronomic phrase "Baalim and
Ashtaroth" again surfaces. "Exclusive worship of Yahweh (v 3) is of the
essence for Dtr.... Baalim and Ashtaroth is a stock expression denoting
Israel's sin in Dtr," explains Ralph W. Klein.[11] He also maintains that
this phrase denotes the singular worship of Baal Hadad and his consort
Ashtart. Klein suggests that the plural form of Ashtoret, rather than
the singular usage of Ashtart, is an apparent dysphemism. In the
Hebrew Bible, the vowels of the Hebrew word *boset*, meaning, "shame,"
are used in Ashtart's name, which are usually deliberately vocalized
as Ashtoreth.[12] The plural usage denoting each of these deities seems
to reflect several manifestations of these same deities.[13] McCarter
suggests that this phrase could be understood to refer broadly not only
to these principal Canaanite deities, but also to the idolatrous worship
of any male or female deity.[14]

In 1 Samuel 7:6 we encounter what appears to be a ritualistic act
of pouring water on the ground, and no exact parallel occurs in the
Hebrew Bible.[15] However, scholars have offered several interpretations
of this act, which have generally centered on the concept of penitence.
For example, Henry Preserved Smith explains that the pouring of water
is "a rite not elsewhere mentioned. It must be symbolic of contrition.
Fasting, which is the second observance mentioned, is elsewhere
expressive of sorrow."[16] Klein agrees with Smith that the practice of
pouring water coupled with the principle of fasting may be meant to
communicate sorrow and repentance. "We read of a command to pour

out the heart like water before Yahweh as an expression of sorrow in Lam. 2:19 (cf. the reference to tears in v. 18)."[17] Raphael Patai maintains that it is a libation to be viewed as an atoning ceremony.[18] S.R. Driver while avoiding the word *libation*, agrees with Patai, noting that this practice is "a symbolic act implying separation from sin: sin was to be cast away as completely as water poured out upon the earth."[19] Finally, Joyce C. Baldwin views the water practice, "as a symbol of the washing away of communal guilt, for which Samuel prayed."[20]

Although the suggestion of penitence may serve as a partial explanation for the practice, the notion of polemic is not mentioned by any of these scholars. However, Philippe Reymond does hint at this possibility when he asks rhetorically,

> Isn't the point of the recitation in the fact that the water is poured out "before Yahweh" and not before Baal? Therefore, if we compare this recitation to that of I Kings 18, one could suppose that at the time of the ceremony of Mispah, as at that of Carmel, however different it may be, Israel would have recognized that Yahweh was her true God; and that, as a consequence, it was from Yahweh and not from Baal it was necessary to obtain rain.[21]

Although Reymond recognizes the plausibility of a water polemic against Baal, his interpretation appears incomplete. We must remember Israel's inherent penitence in this verse. Penitence and polemic combine in this demonstration of loyalty. Israel acknowledges Yahweh as the true source of water, and was willing to pour out, or in other words remove, herself from the sinful worship of the water god Baal-Hadad.

Thus far, this pericope has yielded evidence to support the view that this is an explicit polemic against Baalism. The practice of pouring water before Yahweh immediately follows Israel's putting away of Baal and his consort and indicates the possibility of an implicit water polemic against the storm god (1 Sam. 7:3–6). This notion is strengthened by textual evidence immediately following and concluding this pericope (1 Sam. 7:7–12). In verse 7, the insinuation is that the Philistines surprised the Israelites who were involved with spiritual matters. The Israelites seem to be astonished because possibly they lacked weapons. However, the text relates that the Israelites were not without spiritual weapons, and in their fright they petitioned Samuel to plead to Yahweh in their behalf (1 Sam. 7:8–9). When the Philistines drew near to fight the Israelites, the Lord sent his divine weapons: "Yahweh thundered with a great noise/voice that day upon the Philistines and discomfited them; and they were smitten before Israel" (1 Sam. 7:10). In KTU 1.4.V:8–9, the relationship between storm imagery and the voice of Baal is also attested. The text reads *wtn.qlh.b^{c}rpt srh.l ar$\underline{s}$.brqm*, meaning, "And he gives his voice in the clouds, for the flashing of lightning bolts to the earth." Such literature surely connotes the idea that the lightning flashes are connected with Baal's voice just as thunder is related to Yahweh's utterance. General storm imagery is undoubtedly intended in both cases.

The fact that this literature indicates that Yahweh thundered upon the Philistines and that he *h-m-m* (discomfited) them exposes the hand of DTR. DTR uses this Hebrew verb in the DH storm imagery to destroy the enemies of Yahweh.[22] Furthermore, in the Song of Hannah, the text indicates that "the enemies of Yahweh shall be broken to pieces; out of heaven will he thunder upon them" (1 Sam. 2:10). The Hebrew root for "thundered" is *r-^{c}-m*, the same verb used in 1 Samuel 7:10. Furthermore, the morphology is exactly the same in each of these verses. Such evidence strongly reveals the hand of DTR in the previous statement describing how Yahweh will thunder on his enemies (1 Sam. 2:10) and in the example of its fulfillment (1 Sam. 7:10).

It is important to mention that the Philistines were connected with the worship of Baalism. In the Ugaritic texts Baal is related to Dagon; he is called the son of Dagon eleven times.[23] The Hebrew Bible indicates that Dagon was the principal deity of the Philistines, as attested in the Deuteronomic corpus from Judges 16:21–23 and 1 Samuel 5:1–7; 31:10. Jonas C. Greenfield points out that although we do not know a lot about the Philistine religion, we do know that the Philistines worshipped deities who all had Semitic names and who "had temples to Dagan in Gaza and Ashdod...one to Ashtoreth in Ashkelon (Herodotus I.105) and one to Baal zebub in Ekron (2 Kgs 1:1–16)."[24] The name Baal zebub is most interesting because one of the epithets of Hadad in the Ugaritic texts is Baal zebul, meaning "Prince Baal." The name Baal zebub appears in this text (1 Kgs. 1:1–16) as a dysphemism, as the name does not mean "Prince Baal," but rather the "Lord of the flies." The text continues with the Israelites pursuing the Philistines and smiting them, much as they did Sisera and his Canaanite army (Judg. 4:15–16). Finally, verse twelve indicates that Samuel erected a stone which he named Eben-ezer, which means "stone helper." Such a name in this Deuteronomic literature may allude to Israel's battle against the

Canaanites in the valley of Ajalon when Yahweh sent hail stones or "thunder stones" upon Israel's enemies (Josh. 10:10–11). Perhaps DTR was implying this same notion when he spoke of the "stone helper" which may echo the earlier literature in these verses from Joshua.

The combined evidence of the pericope of 1 Samuel 7:3–12 strongly suggests that these water and storm stories convey a polemic against Baalism. Furthermore, the Deuteronomistic language used in this narrative leaves no doubt that DTR is present.

1 SAMUEL 12:16–19

The second pericope in this chapter is found in 1 Samuel 12:16–19. As a setting for this text, Samuel rehearses some of the righteous acts that Yahweh has performed for Israel since her departure from Egypt (1 Sam. 12:7–8). However, Israel forgot Yahweh and was subsequently brought into bondage (1 Sam. 12:9). With Israel in need of redemption, 1 Samuel 12:10 states in typical Deuteronomic fashion, "And they cried to Yahweh and said, We have sinned, because we have forsaken the Lord, and have served/worshipped Baalim and Ashtaroth, but now deliver us out of the hand of our enemies, and we will serve you."

Yahweh shows his displeasure when Israel later petitions for a king. The text of 1 Samuel 12:16–19 describes Samuel as the spokesman for Yahweh, who uses his power to send thunder and rain.

> (16) Now stand by and see this great thing, which Yahweh will do before your eyes. (17) Is it not wheat harvest today? I will call to Yahweh and he will send thunder and rain; and you will recognize and perceive what a wicked thing you did in the sight of the Lord when you asked for a king. (18) And Samuel called to Yahweh and he sent thunder and rain that day and all of the people were very afraid of Yahweh and Samuel. (19) And all the people said to Samuel, Pray for your servants to Yahweh your God, that we die not, for we have added to all our sins the wickedness of asking for a king.

Concerning the time of this thunderstorm, McCarter, remarks, "The allusion to the wheat harvest marks the season as early summer…when rain rarely fell."[25] Walter Brueggemann states more emphatically that "such a thunderstorm is noteworthy…because it would never happen in that season."[26] Therefore, the literature deliberately portrays Yahweh's as a supernatural event. The word for thunder in verses 17–

18 is *qolot*, which seems to have been deliberately selected here as the word *qol* is attested three times in this chapter and appears to be a Leitwort.[27] This is especially noticeable in verses 14–15 of this chapter where Samuel instructs Israel that her blessings or cursings are associated with Israel's decision to obey or not obey the voice of the Lord. As also evidenced in 1 Samuel 7:10, the thunder is associated with the voice of the Lord and may also be compared to Baal's voice in the storm imagery of KTU 1.4.V:8–9, mentioned in the previous discussion of the 1 Samuel 7:3–12 pericope.

The word for rain in verses 17–18 is *maṭar*. Its occurrence is a blessing; its lack, a curse.[28] The usage of both *qolot* and *maṭar* together is reminiscent of the storm imagery that is encountered in Exodus 9:23–24, where Yahweh sends a terrible storm upon the Egyptians. 1 Samuel 12:18 indicates that the thunder and rain produces the fear of Yahweh in the people.

The use of the word *fear* in verse 18 suggests a covenantal connotation, illustrated when Samuel issues to Israel covenantal consequences in 1 Samuel 12:14–15. The consequences are dependent on Israel's obedience to Yahweh's voice. In fact, Tremper Longman viewed the setting of the 1 Samuel 12:16–19 pericope as a festival of covenant renewal:

> It is our contention that the rainstorm theophany of I Sam. 12:16–19 is not only a sign of Yahweh's omnipotence, but a manifestation of the covenant curse both to illustrate God's displeasure with the people's covenant-breaking request for a king and also to motivate the people to keep the covenant sanctions which Samuel delivered to them (vv 14–15).[29]

In the final verse of the pericope (verse 19), the people ask Samuel to pray to Yahweh that their lives may be spared. Walter Brueggemann associates this fear of death with the fact that such a thunderstorm would destroy the ripe grain.[30] However, the verses that immediately follow indicate that this is a bit short-sighted. 1 Samuel 12:20–21 states:

> (20) But Samuel said to the people, Do not fear. You have indeed done all those wicked things. Do not however, turn away from Yahweh your God, but serve Yahweh with all your heart. (21) Do not turn to follow worthless things, which can neither profit nor save but are worthless.

The Hebrew word here translated as "worthless" is *tohu*, which connotes a feeling of emptiness. It is also used in Deuteronomy 32:10 to represent a desert waste, and in a figurative sense it refers to worthless idols. This understanding provides a possible interpretation of the meaning of "worthless things" in this passage. Perhaps it refers not only to a mortal king whom Israel has requested, but also to Israel's predominant sin of Baalism mentioned in 1 Samuel 12:10 or connects the two: king and royal Baal cult. Interestingly, this word can represent an empty desolate waste which may be associated with the notion that Baalism cannot provide the fertility that it professes, but rather results in desolation and death.

This text reveals that through storm imagery Yahweh has demonstrated his complete control of heaven and earth. It also suggests that Israel does not seem to fear death merely through a destruction of her crops, but she has recognized with awe Yahweh's great power over the earth in all seasons. This may be strengthened by the understanding of the Baal-Mot cycle from Ugarit. In this cycle the Ugaritic texts portray Baal as having power to provide moisture only in the wet season.[31] Throughout the dry season, though, Mot, the personification of death reigns over nature.[32]

The pericope of 1 Samuel 12:16–19 may therefore be seen as an implicit polemic wherein DTR portrays Yahweh's demonstration of his supremacy as God of heaven and earth, the only king whom Israel should seek and who can send storm or moisture in any season. He is the King of kings and Lord of lords at all times and in all seasons. By contrast, the false god Baal is obviously limited to a fixed cycle and void.

2 SAMUEL 22:7–18

The last pertinent text that will be discussed from the Books of Samuel is taken from 2 Samuel 22:7–18. Taken as a whole, this chapter is nearly identical to Psalm 18. According to F.M. Cross and D. N. Freedman, "the importance of this poem for the study of textual transmission can scarcely be overemphasized. No other ancient piece of comparable length appears in parallel texts in the OT."[33] These authors also maintain that both texts, "have been revised and modernized considerably in the course of the transmission, but II Sam 22 preserves a number of archaic readings, which point to a minimal date in the 9th–8th centuries B.C. for the written composition of the poem."[34] They also point out that dating this poem to the 10th century B.C. is not improbable.[35] Mitchell Dahood also provides us with a date similar to Cross and Freedman in suggesting that 2 Samuel 22/Psalm 18, as well as some other early psalms, may have been composed in the Davidic Period.[36] David A. Robertson even goes so far as to place 2 Samuel 22/Psalm 18, and a few very other chapters in the Hebrew Bible between the thirteenth and tenth centuries B.C.[37] In light of this research, this portion of the DH seems more a DTR compilation than a composition, although Hermann Gunkel singularly dates this text to the time of Josiah.[38]

2 Samuel 22 is critical for the purposes of textual analysis, because as Hans Wilhelm Hertzberg states, "this chapter shares with many other descriptions of theophanies a special wealth of catastrophic storm-pictures."[39] The core of the storm imagery occurs in the stratum of text found in verses 7–18:

> (7) In my distress, I called to Yahweh, and cried to my God; and he heard my voice out of his temple, and my cry did enter his ears. (8) Then the earth trembled and quaked, the foundations of heaven shook, because of his [Yahweh's] anger. (9) Smoke ascended from his nostrils, and devouring fire came from his mouth, and coals were kindled from it. (10) He bent the sky and descended, and a heavy cloud was beneath his feet. (11) And he [Yahweh] rode upon a cherub and flew; and he was seen upon the wings of the wind. (12) And he made pavilions of darkness about him, a mass of water and clouds of the skies. (13) In the brightness before him were burned coals of fire. (14) Yahweh thundered from heaven, and the Most High sent forth his voice. (15) And he sent forth arrows and scattered them, lightning and discomfited them. (16) And the channels of the sea were exposed and the foundations of the world were revealed, by the rebuke of Yahweh, at the blast of the breath of his nostrils. (17) He reached down from above, he took me, he drew me out of the mighty waters. (18) He delivered me from my strong enemy, and from those who hated me, for they were too bold for me.

The text describes a Yahwist pleading to his God for deliverance from his enemies; the imagery portrays Yahweh's ability to use the storm to destroy those enemies. Verse 7 introduces the idea that Yahweh communicates from his temple. This may be polemical because Ugaritic literature indicates that Baal sends the voice of storm from his abode upon Mount Zephon (KTU 1.3.III:22–29).[40]

Verses 8 and 9 are reminiscent of Yahweh's storm theophany when he marched out from Mount Seir in Deuteronomy 33:2 and Judges 5:4–5 of the Deuteronomic corpus. Verses 10–12 continue this theme. John Day writes that "the context of this passage is a theophany in a storm, and there can be little doubt that the cherub here was a personification of the storm cloud."[41] These verses again illustrate Yahweh riding the clouds, an idea first attested in the DH in Deuteronomy 33:26, parallel to the epithet of Baal, *rkb ʿrpt*, (Rider of the clouds.)[42]

In verse 13, the storm imagery continues. McCarter translates this verse, "From the brightness before him flared hail and glowing coals."[43] Verse 14 is reminiscent of 1 Samuel 7:10 in which thunder and storm are associated with the voice of Yahweh, as it is with Baal (as mentioned above in the discussion of the pericope of 1 Samuel 7 in KTU 1.4.V:8, *wtn. qlh. bʿrpt*, "And he gives his voice in the clouds").

In verse 15, the word arrows and *baraq*[44] (lightning) parallel each other. Yahweh's weapon, depicted as lightning, is also portrayed as arrows.[45] The text indicates that this lightning discomfited the enemy. The Hebrew verb root (translated "discomfited") here is *h-m-m*, and the use of this Deuteronomic word is a prime piece of evidence that the hand of DTR may have been here.

The root *h-m-m* appears in various forms and is attested a total of 13 times in the Hebrew Bible.[46] Five of these 13 references occur within the Deuteronomic corpus: Deut. 2:15, Judg. 4:15, Josh. 10:10, I Sam. 7:10, and here in 2 Sam. 22:15.[47] However, this root is only attested twice in Psalms: Psalm 144:6 and in the parallel account of 2 Samuel 22:15 and Psalm 18:15. Although each of these accounts contain storm imagery, the latter text includes more details of the storm theophany.

Such evidence suggests that DTR gathered this psalm into the Deuteronomic corpus because it perfectly illustrated the emphasized concept. When introduced in Deuteronomy 7:23 where the Hebrew verbal root *h-w-m* occurs, it relates to *h-m-m*, which may be translated as "to discomfit".[48] Of Israel's enemies the verse states; "And Yahweh your God will deliver them [the enemies] to you, and will discomfit them with a mighty destruction, until they be destroyed." It may also be that DTR used the word *discomfit* in this text and perhaps in other places in order to fit his didactic agenda of polemic against Baalism.

Verses 16–17 provide the literary imagery indicating that while Yahweh uses water and storm to discomfit the enemies of Israel, at the same time he can deliver his covenant people from the *mighty waters,* on the earth, which metaphorically are the enemy as explained in verse 18.

Yahweh's ability to rebuke the mighty waters is most interesting when compared with Baal's ability to rebuke Yam. Furthermore, KTU 1.2.IV:32 we read, *ym. l mt. b^{c}lm.yml[k,* "Yam is dead, Baal will be king." Comparative analysis may suggest that this psalm not only depicts Yahweh's control of Baal's domain, through the subjugation of the waters, but also the superior kingship of Yahweh over Baal. Robert Bruce Chisholm who studied Psalms 18/2 Samuel 22 extensively, concluded his exegetical work with the following statement that sheds light on Yahweh's superior kingship:

> In Psalms 18/2 Samuel 22 David views Yahweh as the incomparable God and king of the universe. More specifically, Yahweh's control over storm and it's elements, as well as his absolute superiority to the surging waters and death itself, demonstrate that he, not Baal, is king. In times of crisis Israel should look to Yahweh for deliverance because only he has the power to protect his people from the hostile forces which seek to destroy them.[49]

My own research and opinion concerning this text echoes Chisholm's statement. The imagery in this literature describes the storm theophany of Yahweh. As with the pericopes of 1 Samuel 7:3–10 and 1 Samuel 12:16–19, in this text, the voice of Yahweh thundering aloud, "I am the King of kings and Lord of lords."

NOTES

1. For excellent information regarding this issue, see Mayes, *The Story of Israel between Settlement and Exile*, 81–105; Robert Polzin, *Samuel and the Deuteronomist: A Literary Study of the Deuteronomic History, Part Two—I Samuel*, (San Francisco: Harper & Row, 1989).

2. Joyce G. Baldwin, "1 and 2 Samuel: An Introduction and Commentary," in *The Tyndale Old Testament Commentaries* (Leicester, England: Intervarsity Press, 1988), 27.

3. Van Seters, *In Search of History*, 359.

4. Henry Preserved Smith, *A Critical and Exegetical Commentary on the Books of Samuel*, vol. 8 of *The International Critical Commentary*, ed. S. R. Driver, Alfred Plummer, and C. A. Briggs (New York: Charles Scribner's Sons, 1899), 50.

5. Ibid., 52.

6. Polzin, *Samuel and the Deuteronomist*, 74. Polzin also provides an excellent list of references which mention the concept of serving Yahweh: Deut. 6:13; 10:12, 20; 11:13; 13:5; 28:47; Josh. 22:5; 24:14, 18, 19, 21, 22, 24; Judg. 2:7; 10:16; 1 Sam. 7:4; 12:14, 20, 24 (ibid., 237 n. 30).

7. Hans Walter Wolff, "The Kerygma of the Deuteronomic Historical Work," trans. Frederick Prussner, in Walter Brueggeman and Hans Walter Wolff, *The Vitality of Old Testament Traditions*, 2d ed. (Atlanta: John Knox Press, 1982), 90.

8. McCarter, *I Samuel*, 142.

9. Ibid., 143.

10. Mayes, *The Story of Israel Between the Settlement and the Exile*, 96–97.

11. Ralph W. Klein, "I Samuel," in vol. 10 of *Word Biblical Commentary*, ed. David A. Hubbard and Glenn W. Barker (Waco, Texas: Word Books, Publisher, 1982), 66.

12. Ibid. McCarter, *I Samuel*, 143, agrees with Klein in stating that Ashtoreth "is probably a deliberate misvocalization to suggest boshet, shame . . ."

13. See Chapter 3, note 53 where this issue was previously discussed.

14. McCarter, *I Samuel*, 143.

15. Klein, "I Samuel," 67.

16. Smith, *A Critical and Exegetical Commentary on the Books of Samuel*, 52.

17. Klein, "I Samuel," 67.

18. Patai, "The 'Control of Rain' in Ancient Palestine," 254. He bases his interpretation on a similar passage in 2 Sam. 23:14–17.

19. S. R. Driver, *Notes on the Hebrew Text and Topography of the Books of Samuel*, 2d ed. (Oxford: Clarendon Press, 1913), 64.

20. Baldwin, "1 and 2 Samuel," 79.

21. Philippe Reymond, "L'eau, sa vie, et signification dans l'Ancien Testament," in vol. 6 of *Supplements to Vetus Testamentum*, ed. G. W. Anderson, P. A. H. De Boer, Millar Burrows, Henri Cazelles, E. Hammershaimb, and Martin Noth (Leiden: E. J. Brill, 1958), 215.

22. See, for example, Deut. 7:23, Josh. 10:10, and Judg. 4:15. For an excellent discussion of the similarities between some of these Deuteronomic stories portraying Yahweh as a warrior, see Peter Weimar, "Die Jahwekriegserzählungen in Exodus 14, Joshua 10, Richter 4 und I Samuel 7," *Biblica* 57 (1976): fasc. 1.

23. Oldenburg, *The Conflict between El and Ba'al in Canaanite Religion*, 46. For more information about the god Dagon, see pp. 47–57 of this text.

24. Jonas C. Greenfield, "Philistines," in vol. 3 of *The Interpreter's Dictionary of the Bible*, ed. George A. Buttrick, Thomas Samuel Kepler, John Knox, Herbert Gordon May, Samuel Terrein, and Emory Stevens Bucker (Nashville: Abingdon Press, 1982), 792.

25. McCarter, *I Samuel*, 216. For a discussion of the climate of Israel, see Scott, "Palestine, Climate of," 621–26.

26. Walter Brueggemann, "First and Second Samuel," in *Interpretation: A Bible Commentary for Teaching and Preaching*, ed. James Luther Mays, Patrick D. Miller, Jr., and Paul J. Achtemeier (Louisville: John Knox Press, 1990), 94.

27. The word *qol*, appears in 1 Sam. 12:1, 14–15.

28. For a listing of the occurrences of *matar* as a blessing or a curse, see Brown et al., *A Hebrew and English Lexicon of the Old Testament*, 564–65.

29. Tremper Longman, III, "I Sam 12:16–19: Divine Omnipotence or Covenant Curse?" *Westminster Theological Journal* 45 (No. 1, 1983): 169.

30. Brueggemann, "First and Second Samuel," 94.

31. There are two opposing views in relation to the Baal-Mot Cycle, which are known as the seasonal or sabbatical cycle. The chief exponent for the sabbatical cycle is Cyrus H. Gordon. His position may be quickly gathered from his article entitled "Sabbatical Cycle or Seasonal Pattern," *Orientalia* 22 (1953): 79–81. Gordon also provides a more thorough discussion of his position in his essay "Canaanite Mythology," in *Mythologies of the Ancient World*, ed. Samuel Noah Kramer (Garden City, N.Y.: Doubleday, 1961), 181–218. The other view, which I prefer, is the seasonal cycle, which is advanced by Kapelrud, *Baal in the Ras Shamra Texts*, 130, who argues that the number seven should be seen in a symbolic rather than a sabbatical sense as it is a holy number and states that "Baal's descent to the nether world [Mot's dominion] had nothing to do with a seven year cycle. It was an event in much closer contact with daily life. It sprang from the changing of the seasons, from the fears and hopes of men whose existence was dependent on the coming of the rain, and on the fertility of fields and animals." This view is followed by Watson, "Mot, The God of Death at Ugarit and in the Old Testament," 195, who states, "the correlation of the successive scenes of the Baal-Mot Cycle with the seasonal pattern...provides strong circumstantial evidence of the annual repetition of the conflict."

32. For an excellent treatise on the god Mot, see Watson, "Mot, The God of Death at Ugarit and in the Old Testament."

33. Frank Moore Cross and David Noel Freedman, "A Royal Song of Thanksgiving: II Samuel-Psalms 18," *Journal of Biblical Literature* 72 (1953): 15.

34. Ibid., 15–16.

35. Ibid., 20.

36. Mitchell A. Dahood, *Psalms I: 1–50*, vol. 16 of *The Anchor Bible*, ed. W. F. Albright and D. N. Freedman (Garden City, N.Y.: Doubleday, 1965–66), xxx.

37. Robertson, *Linguistic Evidence in Dating Early Hebrew Poetry*, ix.

38. Hans-Joachim Kraus, *Psalms 1–59: A Commentary*, trans. Hilton C. Oswald (Minneapolis: Augsburg Publishing House, 1988), 258.

39. Hans Wilhelm Hertzberg, *I & II Samuel: A Commentary*, trans. J. S. Bowden (Philadelphia: Westminster Press, 1964), 395.

40. The idea of comparing Yahweh speaking from his temple as Baal thunders from his abode was derived from Habel, *Yahweh versus Baal*, 85.

41. Day, "The Old Testament Utilization of Language and Imagery Having Parallels in the Baal Mythology of the Ugaritic Texts," 115.

42. Kaiser, "The Ugaritic Pantheon," 268 n. 293, lists an exhaustive list wherein the title *rkb ʿrpt* is used. *UT*, 68:8, 29; ʿnt II:40, III:35, IV:48, 50; 51:III:11, 18, V:122; 76:1, 7; I Aqht 43–44.

43. P. Kyle McCarter, Jr., *II Samuel: A New Translation with Introduction, Notes and Commentary*, vol. 9 of *The Anchor Bible*, ed. W. F. Albright and D. N. Freedman (Garden City, N.Y.: Doubleday, 1984), 453.

44. Note that in Ps. 18:15, *baraq* is in the plural form *beraqim* rather than the singular form of *baraq*.

45. See also Deut. 32:41–42 and Hab. 3:11.

46. Abraham Even-Shoshan, *A New Concordance of the Old Testament Using the Hebrew and Aramaic Text* (Jerusalem: Kiryat Sepher, 1985), 306.

47. Ibid.

48. Brown et al., *A Hebrew and English Lexicon of the Old Testament*, 223, 243.

49. Robert Bruce Chisholm, "An Exegetical and Theological Study of Psalm 18/2 Samuel 22" (Ph.D. diss., Dallas Theological Seminary, 1983), 347.

CHAPTER 5

WATER AND STORM POLEMICS IN THE BOOKS OF KINGS

The corpus of literature in the Books of Kings contains the climatic portion of the Deuteronomic History.[1] The stories of Elijah and Elisha are particularly relevant to this study, because they contain the most abundant collection of polemics against Baalism in the DH.

The issue of polemics against Baal in the Elijah and Elisha narratives has been discussed in a prior work by Leah Bronner entitled *The Stories of Elijah and Elisha as Polemics Against Baal Worship*. As briefly mentioned in the introduction of this dissertation, Bronner's work has received poor reviews. For example, F. C. Fensham emphasized that Bronner creates an "uneasy feeling" as she compares the Ugaritic and Biblical parallel texts.[2] James Battenfield further remarks that "sometimes her points of comparison seem less than compelling."[3] P. A. H. De Boer, in his review of Bronner's work, comments, "It is remarkable how one's own beliefs can expand a text!"[4]

Besides going beyond the evidence available, I emphasize Bronner's failure to examine, in the proper framework of the Deuteronomic History, the material she treats. Furthermore, her bibliography is not complete and she does not rely enough upon the primarily materials available from the Ugaritic texts. Finally, Bronner does not adequately treat the Baalistic core of the polemical material, which centers in the water and storm polemics—the essence of this study.

The hand of DTR is very active throughout the Books of Kings. Prior to the Elijah and Elisha narratives, the Deuteronomist supplies information that leads the reader to believe that syncretism and its devastating effects have crept into Israel, beginning with the court and then spreading to the common people.

For example, the text relates Solomon's marriages to foreign wives to the growth of idolatrous practices which resulted in the division of the kingdom (1 Kgs. 11:1–13). Such a division led to the appointment of Jeroboam, the son of Nebat, as king of the Northern Kingdom. In order to keep his people from traveling to the Southern Kingdom where the temple was located, he had two golden calves or young bulls[5] erected: he placed one in Dan and the other in Bethel. These served to remind the Israelites of their prior deliverance (1 Kgs. 12:28–29).[6] Although the calves or young bulls were probably initially a pedestal for Yahweh,[7] they were also a platform for the syncretic dissemination of Baalism, since the bull or calf was closely associated with the Baalistic cult. In fact, H. Th. Obbink sensibly argues that the cultic figure was borrowed from the cult of Baal.[8] Walter J. Harrelson concludes that "the bull was entirely too apt a symbol of fertility long to remain unrelated to Canaanite cult practices and religious understandings."[9] The erection of these images led to Jeroboam's infamy. DTR consistently notes that the subsequent kings of the Northern Kingdom followed after the sin of Jeroboam, which became a symbol to describe wickedness par excellence. Furthermore, this act "became the sin of the house of Jeroboam to cause it to disappear and to destroy it from the face of the earth" (1 Kgs. 13:34). Frank Moore Cross emphatically argues that DTR stressed that above all, "the crucial event in the history of the Northern Kingdom was the sin of Jeroboam."[10]

The syncretic mixture of Yahwism and Baalism, which was furthered by Jeroboam's idolatrous Baalistic platform, was at its zenith during the period of the Omri Dynasty which followed. According to the text, Omri purchased the hill Samaria, and from there he reigned in wickedness, surpassing the wickedness of all the kings who came before him as he walked in the ways of Jeroboam (1 Kgs. 16:24–26). Then Omri died and Ahab, his son, reigned in his stead (1 Kgs. 16:28). The verses that follow indict Ahab as the most wicked king in Israel. He not only followed in the ways of Jeroboam, but he also married Jezebel, a daughter of the Phoenician King Ethbaal,[11] and erected an altar for Baal in Samaria and worshipped him. Ahab made a sacred post (asherah) and angered Yahweh more than any of the kings of Israel who reigned before him (1 Kgs. 16:29–33). Robert L. Cohn notes that "the deuteronomic summary of Ahab's reign in I Kgs. 16:29–33 serves as a prologue to the Elijah narrative because it identifies the issue with which Elijah must deal: Ahab's patronage of Baal."[12] Baalism in general is in fact the focus, not only Ahab's patronage of Baal, but also that of his idolatrous wife Jezebel and the vast majority of his kingdom.

1 KINGS 17–19

The material in 1 Kings 17–19 will now be analyzed. This stratum of the Book of Kings contains the climax of water and storm polemics against Baalism, not only in the Book of Kings and the DH, but also within the Hebrew Bible as a whole. Cohn concluded of this portion of Kings, "Only 1 Kings 17–19 within the Elijah cycle has as its central theme the battle for the establishment of the exclusive worship of Yahweh against the forces of Baal."[13] On the role of DTR in these chapters, F. C. Fensham remarked that the Deuteronomist's role in 1 Kings 17–19 is not clear.[14] Alan J. Hauser suggested that "the writer has carefully selected his sources and has trimmed and focused them to present in dramatic fashion the power of Yahweh as the victorious God of life."[15]

As mentioned above, 1 Kings 16:29–33 is a polemical prologue to the Elijah narrative which follows in 1 Kings 17–19. In the introductory verse in 1 Kings 17:1, Elijah said to Ahab, "As Yahweh lives, the God of Israel whom I serve, there will be no dew or rain these years, but according to my word." Just so, the Ugaritic text of KTU 1.19.I:42–46 manifests Baal's supposed control of dew and rain:

> Seven years shall Baal fail,
> Eight the rider of clouds.
> There shall be no dew, no rain
> No surging of the deeps,
> Neither the goodness of Baal's voice

In light of this background, it seems most reasonable to argue that our verse is indeed a water/storm polemic against Baal.

The literature in 1 Kings 18:1 reveals that Yahweh told Elijah in the third year of this drought to "Go, appear before Ahab; then I will send rain upon the earth." The severity of this drought is historically supported by Josephus (Antiq. VIII.xiii.2), who recounts the records of Menander of Ephesus, that during the reign of Ethbaal and in the days of Ahab there was a famine that lasted for about a year. However, Menander also adds that when Ethbaal made supplications (undoubtedly to Baal), the drought ended.[16] While Josephus quotes Menander as writing that the drought lasted about a year, the New Testament indicates that the famine lasted three-and-a-half years.[17] Regardless of the duration of the drought, the notion of a severe famine in the land during this time suggests an element of historicity.

The literature in 1 Kings 18 heightens the portrayal of the harshness of the famine, for the text indicates not only the severity of the drought in Samaria (1 Kgs. 18:2), but also reveals that it was so intense that even King Ahab joined his servant Obadiah in searching the entire country for a water source (1 Kgs. 18:3–5). The land is divided between them and each goes alone in a different direction. Suddenly Obadiah encounters Elijah, who tells him to return to Ahab to inform him that "Elijah is here" (1 Kgs. 18:6–11). Upon seeing Elijah, Ahab refers to him as an ʿokher ("troubler") of Israel (1 Kgs. 18:17). Elijah retorts, "I haven't troubled Israel, but you and your father's house in that you have abandoned the commandments of Yahweh and gone after the Baalim" (1 Kgs. 18:18). Here, in 1 Kings 18:18 Elijah launches into an obvious polemical proclamation against Baal worship, while at the same time revealing his monotheistic message of Yahweh. Referring to the deliberate use of the word Baalim in this verse, C. F. Burney, while acknowledging that the reference is indeed to the Canaanite god Baal, suggests, "Some contempt is conveyed by the use of the plural as contrasted with the one Yahweh."[18] This is strengthened by the fact that in the following verse the singular name Baal is used, rather than the plural word Baalim.

The encounter between Ahab and Elijah leads to a climactic confrontation to determine whether Yahweh or Baal controls the rain water. Elijah boldly challenges Ahab in verse 19, "Now send and gather to me all Israel to Mount Carmel and the four hundred and fifty prophets of Baal and the four hundred prophets of Asherah, who eat at Jezebel's table" (1 Kgs. 18:19).

This showdown on Mount Carmel is interesting for several reasons. One is that at the time of this confrontation, Mount Carmel was situated exactly on the border of Israel and Phoenicia. This is useful information, for Jezebel, a zealous advocate of Baal, had advanced the penetration of Baalism into Israel from her homeland in Phoenicia. Perhaps this location was selected because it was the most neutral position for such an encounter between the god of each land.

Second, Otto Eissfeldt points out that this very fertile area would have been a great showcase for the fruits of the worship of Baal.[19] In fact, the Hebrew word *Karmel* actually means "garden land."[20] Furthermore, Mount Carmel is used in the Hebrew Bible as an image for fertility as well as beauty.[21] Finally, an inscription dated to 841 B.C. and attributed to Shalmaneser III has been found, evidence that Mount Carmel was called Mount *Ba'li-ra'si* "Baal of the headland."[22] The fact that the inscription dates to the ninth century B.C. suggests that Mount Carmel was referred to as Baal's mountain or domain during the time of Elijah's showdown with the priests of Baal. Stephen Szikszai writes, "The details of the contest of Mount Carmel reveal the growth of the miraculous element in the tradition, but the essential historicity of the contest can hardly be denied."[23]

Ahab next summoned the people and prophets of Israel to Mount Carmel (1 Kgs. 18:20), and when all were gathered, Elijah emphatically inquired, "'How long are you going to keep hopping between two branches? If Yahweh is God follow him; and if Baal, follow him!' But the people did not answer him" (I Kgs. 18:21). The idea is strongly transmitted that the influence of Baalism had reached a peak in Israel and that it needed to be confronted head on. Gerhard von Rad confirms, "What had always been a danger now became an acute one."[24] Eakin maintains that this narrative "was not only the initial case of overt conflict, but this conflict so aroused the devotees of Yahwism that a steady polemic was henceforth raised against the Baalization of Yahwism in both Israel and Judah. This polemical voice came to a climax in the writing of the Deuteronomic historians."[25]

The writer portrays Elijah as teaching that Yahwism and Baalism were absolutely incompatible. Von Rad further suggests that Elijah's exaction must have come as a shock to his people, because "[he] viewed the matter as a case of either-or."[26] However, this literature seems to be arranged so as to echo the words of Joshua, "Choose you this day whom you will serve" (Josh. 24:15).

Further, in this climatic contest, the odds against Elijah are 450 to 1, he being Yahweh's only remaining prophet in the land to face the 450 prophets of Baal (1 Kgs. 18:22). Such a statement appears to be hyperbole, since Obadiah is said to have hid one hundred prophets of Yahweh in a cave (1 Kgs. 18:4). Also 1 Kings 22:6 relates that following this event, King Ahab consulted about four hundred Yahwistic prophets.[27]

The contest is to be decided by which god will answer by sending fire to consume a sacrificial bull (1 Kgs. 18:22–25). The prophets of Baal plead from sun-up until high noon for Baal to answer them, but there is no reply (1 Kgs. 18:26). Elijah mocks them, and finally, in desperation they cut themselves, letting the blood flow, yet to no avail (1 Kgs. 18:27–29). This act of letting the blood drip may have been a form of imitative magic wherein the life-giving force of the blood typifies the life-giving element of the rain so desperately needed.[28]

Elijah then asks all the people to draw near him as he repairs the altar of Yahweh that was broken down (1 Kgs. 18:30).[29] He re-erects the altar, using twelve stones to symbolize the twelve tribes of Israel, and digs a trench around it (1 Kgs. 18:31–32). Elijah then positions the wood, lays the sacrificial bull on the altar, and orders four barrels of water to be poured on the wood, which is then repeated three times (1 Kgs. 18:33–34). The mention of the twelve stones as symbolic of the twelve tribes further suggests that the four barrels of water poured three different times are also symbolic. Perhaps one could speculate that the number four represents the four corners of the earth or all the land of Israel; and the number three symbolizes the three years of drought, as specified in the text. Water would soon be poured over all the land of Israel, which had suffered from this severe famine for three years.[30] Raphael Patai not only concurs that the number three symbolizes the three years of drought but also adds that this pouring out of water is the most common form of sympathetic magic regarding rain making.[31] However, this does not appear to be the writer's main objective; rather the writer attempts to convey the power of Yahweh, as further evidenced in the theophany of this text. Perhaps he does so through exaggerating the task by wetting the wood.

After the water was poured upon the altar, Elijah prayed to Yahweh, "'Answer me O Yahweh, Answer me, that this people may know that you Yahweh are God...' Then fire from Yahweh descended and consumed the burnt offering, and the wood, and the stones, and the dust, and licked up the water that was in the trench" (1 Kgs. 18:35–38). Russell Gregory writes, "Two contrasting elements, one the nemesis of drought, one the conqueror of drought, appear in this section."[32] However, such a supernatural fire attending this theophany may also be viewed as lightning, which seems to be what the literature tries to convey in this episode. Patai also suggests that the fire may have been lightning. Gray more confidently asserts that it was "the lightning which ignited the sacrifice." On the other hand, A. Lucas argues that Elijah poured an inflammable liquid on the altar and compares his view to a story from 2 Maccabees 1:19–22. R. H. Kennett maintains that the fire was kindled by a mirror which reflected the rays of the sun.[33] However, these opinions appear to be very weak, since the Yahwistic literature is designed to emphasize Yahweh's superior power over Baal.

The text evidences that this was a theophany to be viewed as a determining factor in the history of Israel. Following this theophany the people fell on their faces and proclaimed, "Yahweh, he is God, Yahweh he is God" (1 Kgs. 18:39). They not only proclaimed the name of Yahweh, but also put an end to the lives of the prophets of Baal, as Elijah ordered (1 Kgs. 18:40).

1 Kings 18:41 supports the assertion that it was lightning that fell from heaven on this occasion. Elijah tells Ahab to arise because he hears the sound of approaching rain. Elijah then sends his servant to the sea seven times to look for the signs of approaching rain. On the completion of his seventh[34] trip, the servant tells Elijah that a cloud is approaching from the west (1 Kgs. 18:42–44). The text then adds: "Meanwhile the sky grew black with clouds; there was wind, and a great rain" (1 Kgs. 18:45).

Lightning and rain must be viewed together in this pericope if one is to understand the true meaning of the text. On this issue Nicholas J. Tromp reasons,

> We must also assent to the statement that the narra-
> tive is dealing with rain, and this for several reasons.
> If the fire is indeed to be understood as lightning, it
> has been correctly remarked that in the climate of the
> country this is naturally followed by rain. The
> connection between the two is also obvious in that
> Baal was considered as the god of both lightning and
> rain; the contest proves that Yahweh has an exclusive
> claim to this title.[35]

The critical issue here is to answer the question of who controls the water, Yahweh or Baal. In this polemical account (which Tromp suggests DTR is relating to his day),[36] Baal is portrayed again as a usurper of Yahweh's domain. The Ugaritic literature makes Baal's ability to control the elements of rain and storm continually evident. For example KTU 1.4.V:6–9 reads:

The time for his rain Baal is appointing,

the time for moisture;
And he gives his voice in the clouds,
for the flashing of lightning-bolts to the earth.

The conclusion to this narrative and polemic occurs in 1 Kings 19, with the implication that although Elijah had turned the hearts of the assembled Israelites back to Yahweh, the heart of Jezebel only grew harder. This becomes clear when the text informs us that when Ahab told Jezebel of the events on Mount Carmel, Jezebel sent a messenger to Elijah to tell him she had sworn an oath that she would do to him as he had done to her prophets of Baal (1 Kgs. 19:1–2).[37] This news depresses Elijah to the point that he wants to die. An angel then appears and strengthens him with food and drink, to sustain him for forty days as he journeys to Mount Horeb (1 Kgs. 19:3–8).[38] The fact that Elijah journeys south to the abode of Yahweh in Mount Horeb suggests a polemical element, made apparent through a reminder that Baal is said to dwell on Mount Saphon, which lies in the opposite direction in the north—a direct antithesis.[39]

When Elijah reaches Mount Horeb, the voice of the Lord asks why he is there (1 Kgs. 19:9). Elijah recounts how the children of Israel have strayed and even killed Yahweh's prophets and how his life is being sought (1 Kgs. 19:10). In, 1 Kings 19:11–12 Yahweh instructs Elijah to stand upon the mount before him. The text states,

> (11) And behold Yahweh passed by, and a great and strong wind tore apart the mountains and shattered the rocks before Yahweh; but Yahweh was not in the wind; after the wind an earthquake, but Yahweh was not in the earthquake. (12) And after the earthquake a fire; but Yahweh was not in the fire; and after the fire a still small voice.

Cross sees in these verses three elements of the storm theophany: wind, quaking, and fire [lightning]. He further suggests that when these elements are used here, in each case we should probably translate "Yahweh was no longer in the storm."[40] A. S. Peake rhetorically asks, "Was then this display of Nature's stupendous forces a mockery, eviscerated of the Divine presence with which in earlier days they had been charged? No, for while God himself is not in them they are the harbingers of His coming."[41] Cohn further explains, "The author thus creates the most dramatic of contrasts between the silence of Baal and the voice of Yahweh which is beyond not within the elements of nature that Baal is believed to control."[42] Yahweh is here portrayed as having no bounds; he is to be viewed as the author of creation who reigns above and beyond all things. The pericope of 1 Kings 17–19 thus illustrates Baal's obvious limitations, and this is perhaps further contrasted by the idea that while Baal appears deaf and dumb on Mount Carmel, the epitome of nature in its most fructified state, Yahweh can hear and speak, not only from the fertile region of Carmel, but also from the desert region of Horeb and from anywhere for that matter.

This polemical cycle concludes with information that Elijah is not completely alone in his stand against Baalism as 7,000 Israelites have not embraced Baalism (1 Kgs. 19:18). The implication is that although Elijah has won a battle against Baal on Mount Carmel he surely has not won the war against Baalism in Israel. Eakin points out that Elijah's contribution was that he brought a distinct clarity to Yahwism.[43] H. H. Rowley went so far as to say that "without Moses the religion of Yahwism as it figured in the Old Testament would never have been born. Without Elijah it would have died."[44]

The editorial hand of DTR is apparent in the verses that follow. The implication is that Elijah's attack against Baalism was to be carried out largely by Israel's future king (Jehu), and her future prophet (Elisha), whom Elijah was instructed by Yahweh to anoint (1 Kgs. 19:15–17). This assertion is later verified in 2 Kings 2–10 of the DH.

2 KINGS 1:1–18

The death of Ahab[45] (1 Kgs. 22:37) brought his son Ahaziah to the throne, and he angered Yahweh as his father had done when he followed the idolatrous ways of Jeroboam and worshipped Baal (1 Kgs. 22:51–53). Ahaziah was injured when he fell through a lattice in his upper chamber in Samaria; therefore, he sent messengers to inquire of Baal-zebub, the god of Ekron, whether or not he would recover from his injury (2 Kgs. 1:2). An angel of Yahweh was then sent to tell Elijah to meet these messengers and to ask them, "Is there no God in Israel that you go to inquire of the Baal-zebub, the God of Ekron?" (2 Kgs. 1:3). As Yahweh's spokesman, Elijah informs the messengers that Ahaziah will not rise from his bed, but will die (2 Kgs. 1:4).

The usage of the name Baal-zebub, meaning "Lord of the Flies," is a dysphemism which brings disrepute to Baal's reputation. It is a deliberate distortion of *b⁽c⁾l zbl*, which, as mentioned, is an epithet for

Hadad that means "Lord Prince."[46] This parody serves to signal that later editors took the text as an obvious polemic against Baal.

Next, when the messengers return to Ahaziah and inform him of their encounter with Elijah and of his prophetic message, Ahaziah sends a group of fifty men led by a captain to apprehend Elijah (2 Kgs. 1:5–9). The captain calls to Elijah, who is positioned on a hill, and says to him, "Man of God, the king said come down!" (2 Kgs. 1:9). Elijah answers the captain, "If I be a man of God, then let fire come down from heaven and consume you with your fifty men. And fire from heaven descended and consumed him and his fifty" (2 Kgs. 1:10).[47] The narrative also informs us that this pattern repeats when Ahaziah sends a second captain with his fifty, who are likewise consumed (2 Kgs. 1:11–12).

A third captain is then sent, who pleads for Elijah to descend (rather than the fire) so that his life and the lives of his fifty would be spared and not consumed like those bands who have gone before him (2 Kgs. 1:13). The text then indicates that Yahweh sends an angel to inform Elijah that he should descend with him and meet the king (2 Kgs. 1:15). Upon meeting Ahaziah, Elijah says, "Thus says Yahweh, 'Because you sent messengers to inquire of Baal-zebub, the god of Ekron, as if there were no God in Israel whose word you could inquire of, you will not rise from off your bed which you are lying upon, but you will die. So he died according to the word of Yahweh" (2 Kgs. 1:16–17).

This statement reinforces the notion that this narrative is an explicit polemic against Baal. Furthermore, as we consider the blazing lightning that descends in the Mount Carmel pericope (1 Kgs. 18), the text implies that the fire that consumed these men was also lightning.[48] This was to be the sign that Elijah was truly Yahweh's representative, "a man of God." In this pericope we again encounter Yahweh harnessing one of the elements that Baal is said to control in order to punish those who worship him. This sign must be considered as another apparent storm polemic against Baalism.

2 KINGS 2:8–15

In this narrative we encounter the transition of prophetic authority from Elijah to Elisha. Yahweh affirms his choice of Elisha to succeed Elijah by parting the Jordan River. This is very similar to the sign given when the Jordan was parted for Joshua. Joshua 3 indicates that just as Yahweh's power was made manifest through Moses in the separation of the Red Sea, so it would be made known through Joshua's parting of the Jordan.[49]

The literature in this chapter points out that Elijah smote the river with his mantle and that the waters were divided such that both Elijah and Elisha passed through the Jordan on dry ground (2 Kgs. 2:8). Later, as they went on their way, a chariot of fire with fiery horses appeared and suddenly Elijah was taken in a whirlwind (storm)[50] up into heaven (2 Kgs. 2:11). James R. Battenfield explains: "Elijah could be taken any number of ways. But a 'chariot of fire' is YHWH's chosen conveyance—evidently to refute Baalism."[51] This manifestation clearly reveals elements of a storm theophany as Elijah ascends in a whirlwind of storm and rides the heavens in a chariot of fire. This is reminiscent of Baal, who as previously noted is occasionally referred to by the epithet *rkb ʿrpt*, "Rider of the Clouds."

Elisha then picked up Elijah's mantle, which had fallen to the ground, and with it smote the Jordan and asked, "Where is Yahweh, the God of Elijah? And when he too struck the waters, they divided to each side and Elisha crossed over" (2 Kgs. 2:13–14). The text clearly depicts the act of parting the waters as the sign that Yahweh's power has indeed been passed to Elisha. In addition, this is another water polemic against Baal. As already noted from KTU 1.2.IV:22–28,[52] Baal is said to have smitten and conquered Judge River with his two weapons made for him by Kothar-wa-Hasis, the craftsman of the gods. In like manner, Yahweh has once again made known his ability to part the waters through the instrumentality of his prophets, who act in his name and through his power and authority.

2 KINGS 2:19-22

In this short account, Elisha casts salt into a bitter spring in Jericho in order to heal the water source that issues forth from beneath the earth (2 Kgs. 2:19-21).[53] When he does so, he also declares, "Thus said Yahweh: I have healed these waters; there will not come from it any more death and bereavement" (2 Kgs. 2:21). The text indicates that the spring was cured and DTR also emphasizes the notion these waters are healed *until this day* (2 Kgs. 2:22, emphasis added).

Although the Ugaritic material is silent in regard to Baal's specific ability to heal springs, there is still the notion of Baal's comprehensive capacity to control the waters above the earth, upon the

earth, and those that spring up from beneath the earth. This concept
seems apparent not only in the texts, but also in a limestone stele
excavated from Ras Shamra.[54] Concerning the imagery of this stele,
Bronner writes,

> It depicts Baal standing on what might be either
> heaven or the earth. He brandishes a club in one
> hand, and holds a stylized thunderbolt ending in a
> spear in the other. Baal is standing on what appears
> as undulating lines separated by three horizontal
> lines. These lines could be regarded as representing
> him as a celestial god, treading the heavenly ocean or
> waters that are beyond the firmament. . . . However,
> the lines beneath the feet of Baal can be given a
> different and perhaps a more convincing interpreta-
> tion. The three horizontal lines upon which the god
> stands symbolize the earth. Of the two undulating
> lines underneath the feet of Baal, one represents the
> sea; the other, less boldly traced, the waters under the
> earth.[55]

Battenfield maintains that in this stele, "Baal is depicted as (1)
treading on the earth and (2) ruling over the waters on and beneath
the earth (thus also over underground springs and fountains)."[56] It
may be more accurate to view this stele somewhat differently:
Perhaps the two rippling lines upon which Baal stands represent
water. Conceivably, the three horizontal lines that separate these two
undulating lines may distinguish the waters above, upon, and beneath
the earth. Such an interpretation fits not only the Ugaritic portrait of
Baal, but also is evidenced in the DH where Yahweh is depicted as
Lord of heaven and earth, which seems to include all that lies beneath
and beyond.

2 KINGS 3:1-27

In this narrative the subject of waters that lie beneath the earth
again surfaces. This chapter commences with Jehoram, son of Ahab,
now on the throne (2 Kgs. 3:1). The writer also informs us that
although Jehoram continues in the sins of Jeroboam (meaning the
idolatrous calves remained), he is not as evil as Ahab because he has
removed the *mazzebat ha-ba'al* stele that his father had erected in
Samaria (2 Kgs. 3:2-3).

The water polemic emerges at the time of the death of Ahab
when Moab revolts against Israel (2 Kgs. 3:5). Jehoram rallies the

kings of Edom and Judah to combine their forces, and the three allied forces journey for seven days on the road through the wilderness of Edom. Their supply of water for the army and the animals is exhausted (2 Kgs. 3:6-9). Elisha is petitioned by the kings of Israel and Judah; he agrees to provide water through his powers as a Yahwist prophet, not for the sake of Jehoram, but for the benefit of Jehoshapat, king of Judah (2 Kgs. 3:11-14). Elisha then requests a musician, and as the minstrel plays, the power of Yahweh comes upon Elisha (2 Kgs. 3:15). Elisha then says, "Thus said Yahweh, Make [Dig] this wadi full of ditches. For thus said Yahweh: You shall see no wind, you will see no rain, yet that wadi will be filled with water, and you and your cattle and your animals will drink" (2 Kgs. 3:16-17).

Battenfield points out that the Aqht literature from Ugarit provides a cognate text, which indicates that music is provided when Baal provides drink.[57] His translation is taken from KTU 1.17.VI:30-32:

> Even as Baal, when he gives life,
> entertains the living,
> entertains and gives him to drink,
> and the lovely one sings and croons over him
> and responds to him.[58]

The water provided for this coalition in 2 Kings 3 is depicted as coming from beneath the earth. KTU 1.19.I:45-46 indicates that when Baal fails, there will be "no surging of the deeps, neither the goodness of Baal's voice." The Ugaritic word here translated as "deeps" is *thmtm*, the dual form of *thm*, "deep." These Hebrew cognate words are transliterated as *tehom*, most often translated as "deep"; and *tehomot*, its plural form, as "deeps." However, these words are also used in the Hebrew Bible to depict various forms of subterranean waters. For example, *tehomot* is used in Deuteronomy 8:7, where the covenant land of Israel is described as an abundant water source, and could be translated as "deeps," or better yet, "fountains" or "springs" (Deut. 8:7).[59]

The text later records that Elisha informs this coalition that Yahweh will perform an even greater act than the miraculous provision of water: he will deliver the Moabites into their hand (2 Kgs. 3:18). When the Moabites hear of the coalition formed against them, they rise up early in the morning when the sun is shining upon the waters. This causes the water to appear to be red, and the Moabites perceive it as blood shed by the coalition fighting amongst themselves.

The Moabites soon move towards the camp of Israel only to learn that they have been deceived by the appearance of the water; and as a result, their blood is shed there, rather than the blood of the coalition army, as they had falsely supposed (2 Kgs. 3:21-24).

In this chapter we again witness the pattern first established by DTR in the DH from the material in Deuteronomy 32-33, where Yahweh's provision and power are portrayed. We also witness here the common thread in the DH as a whole: the element of storm, and in this case water, is used to bless Yahweh's allies and at the same time curse his foes.

2 KINGS 5:1-19

In the Elisha material discussed thus far, we have seen Yahweh's power to partition (2 Kgs. 2:8-14), provide (2 Kgs. 3:17, 22) and heal water (2 Kgs. 2:19-22). In this narrative we encounter Yahweh's ability to heal through the element of water. This text recounts the story of Naaman, a leper who commands the army of Aram (2 Kgs. 5:1). A young girl has told Naaman of Elisha's ability to cure leprosy. He therefore informs the king of Aram, who sends a letter to the king of Israel requesting that he see to it that Naaman be cured of his disease. The king of Israel is perplexed by this request, but when Elisha hears of it, he asks that Naaman be sent to him so that Naaman may know that there is a prophet in Israel (2 Kgs. 5:2-8). Elisha sends a messenger to tell Naaman that he can be cured if he will wash himself in the Jordan River seven times. Naaman is offended that Elisha would choose to send a messenger rather than meeting with him and invoking the name of his God Yahweh by name. Furthermore, Naaman is bothered by the specific instruction to bathe in the Jordan River (2 Kgs. 2:10-11). He declares, "Are not the Abana and Pharpar, the rivers of Damascus, better than all the waters of Israel? Couldn't I wash in them and be clean?" (2 Kgs. 5:12). He stomps off in a rage, but is later persuaded by his servants to immerse himself in the Jordan as Elisha specifically instructed him. As a result the text relates that Naaman is cured (2 Kgs. 5:12–14). Naaman then returns to Elisha, "the man of God," and states in the company of his men, "Now I know that there is no God in all the earth, except Israel" (2 Kgs. 5:15). Naaman presses Elisha to receive gifts from him, but Elisha refuses (2 Kgs. 5:15-16). Naaman concludes:

> (17) Then at least let your servant have two mule-
> loads of earth; for your servant will never again offer

up burnt offering of sacrifice to any god, except Yahweh.[60] (18) But may Yahweh pardon your servant in this; that when my master enters the temple of Rimmon to bow in worship there, and he is leaning on my hand so that I must bow in the temple of Rimmon, when I bow in the temple of Rimmon, may Yahweh forgive your servant for this thing. (19) And he [Elisha] replied to him, "Go in peace."

Mordechai Cogan and Hayim Tadmor explain that *Rimmon* "is an appellative of Hadad, the god of storm and thunder, and derives from the [Akkadian] root *r m m*, to thunder."[61] John Gray adds, "The identity of Rimmon with Hadad and his significance in the religion of the Syrians of Damascus is confirmed by the fact that 'Hadad' occurs as an element in the theophoric name Ben-Hadad, borne by several kings of Syria, and Tabrimmon, the father of Ben-Hadad (1 Kgs. 15:18)."[62] Gray also suggests that the mourning for Hadadrimmon mentioned in Zechariah 12:11 is probably a rite related to the Ugaritic mythic literature in which Anat mourns for Baal.[63]

The identification of the temple of Rimmon with Hadad reveals a polemical element against Baal in this story. This understanding, combined with the prior knowledge that Naaman is healed by Yahweh's prophet through the instrumentality of river water (which Baal is said to solely control), after which he declares that Yahweh is the only God in all earth, makes apparent the nature of this pericope as a polemic against Baalism with water at its center.

2 KINGS 6:1-7

These verses hint at another water polemic. Elisha is persuaded by his servants to go to the Jordan River to cut timber for additional shelter that is needed (2 Kgs. 6:1-4). The text then reads,

(5) As one of them was felling a beam, the iron ax head dropped into the water. And he cried out and said, "Oh my master, it was a borrowed one." (6) And the man of God asked, "Where did it fall?" He showed him the place; and he cut down a stick and threw it in, and made the ax head float. (7) And he [Elisha] said "Pick it up," and he reached out and picked it up.

Although there is no mention of Baal in this pericope, the fact that Elisha again exercises his divine power over water must at least be recognized. Considered in light of the literature's portrayal of the deep penetration of Baalism into Israel and the many stories regarding water and storm in the lives of Elijah and Elisha, the implication is that this narrative relates to all these other water stories. The implication of another water polemic aimed at Baalism is clear.

2 KINGS 6:24-8:1

2 Kings 6:24-25 describe a great famine in Samaria: Ben Hadad, the king of Syria, has besieged the city and garnered the food supply already limited due to a drought. The text also implies that the king of Israel considered Elisha the cause of the drought (2 Kgs. 6:31). Perhaps the text hints that the king of Israel perceives that Elisha has sealed the heavens, as Elijah had done.[64]

This lends credence to the view that not only was there a famine in Samaria, heightened by the siege of the Syrian army, but there was also a drought that affected the land of Israel as well. In fact, the text later specifies that the Shunammite woman whose son Elisha had healed was warned to flee with her family from Israel because Yahweh had called for a severe famine, that had already commenced and would last a total of seven years (2 Kgs. 8:1). Therefore, she and her family left Israel and lived for the next seven years in the land of the Philistines (2 Kgs. 8:2). Furthermore, as early as 2 Kings 4:38, there is an indication that Elisha has witnessed a drought in the land of Israel that seems very likely to be the seven-year drought described above.

2 Kings 7:1 points out that Elisha foretold in the name of Yahweh that there would be temporary relief from Samaria's food problems (although it does not indicate that the drought would soon end).[65] One of the king's officer's asked, "Behold if Yahweh were to make windows in the sky, would this thing even be?" (2 Kgs. 7:2).

Relevant to this pericope is not only the mention of the severe drought that Yahweh has called for, but also the point that if Yahweh were to make windows in the sky, the famine would cease. The Ugaritic literature implies that Baal has a window in his house from which he pours water, a window constructed by the craftsman god Kothar-wa-Hasis, who declared the following words, as recorded in KTU 1.4.VII:25b–29:

> Let a window be opened in the house
> An opening in the midst of the palace
> Baal opened clefts of the clouds
> Baal gave his holy voice

Concerning the implication of rain water being poured out from the ⁾*urbt* (window), which Johannes C. de Moor translates as *air hole,* he explains,

> Although the rain itself is not mentioned expressly in our passage it has long been suspected that the opening of the air-hole (⁾*urbt*) should be interpreted as the opening of the floodgates of heaven to let through the shower of Baʿlu. This is suggested not only by the obvious identification of the air-hole with a rift in the clouds (*bdqt ʿrpt*) and by the thundering of *Baʿlu* which implies rain, but also by the fact that according to the Israelites the rain descended through air-holes (⁾*arubbot*) in the firmament.[66]

The severe famine called for by Yahweh, as well as the mention of his windows in the sky, again provides evidence of another storm and water polemic against Baal.

Aftermath

Elisha's statement that Yahweh had called for a famine that would last seven years (2 Kgs. 8:1) may be viewed as a symbol for the eminent destruction of the two kingdoms of Israel. The concluding chapters of the Books of Kings at the end of the DH reveal that the water and storm polemics, which reached their peak in the Elijah and Elisha stories, subside. The fact that there are more water and storm polemics during the time of Elijah and Elisha is most interesting when it is recognized that the literature reflects that this occurred during the time that Ahab and especially Jezebel caused Baal worship to reach its zenith in Israel. Furthermore, there may be a correlation between the death of Ahab and Jezebel and the subsiding of the water and storm polemics which occur simultaneously. DTR then conveys the notion that Israel has seen enough of Yahweh's superior power over Baal, especially through the polemical usage of water and storm literature. In the culmination of the DH (2 Kgs. 9-25), DTR sums up the historical events that led to the disastrous consequences that befell the two kingdoms, a direct result of their apostasy to Baalism.

The first event occurs in the reign of Jehu, king of Israel. Jehu was specifically set apart to perform the task of destroying the house of Ahab, which was steeped in Baal worship (2 Kgs. 9:6-7). The text indicates that Jehu saw to it that Jezebel was slain (2 Kgs. 9:30-36) along with the seventy sons of Ahab in Samaria (2 Kgs. 10:7). Jehu also tricked the followers of Baal by inviting them to a solemn feast in the temple of Baal[67] that resulted in their death (2 Kgs. 10:18-25). DTR mentions that Jehu's servants brought out the pillars of Baal from the temple and destroyed them "until this day" (2 Kgs. 10:26-27). The text then says, "Thus Jehu destroyed Baal from Israel. However, he did not turn away from the sinful objects by which Jeroboam son of Nebat had caused Israel to sin, namely, the golden calves at Bethel and Dan" (2 Kgs. 10:28-29). This Deuteronomic editorial implies that although Jehu may have destroyed the physical image of Baal in the land for a time, he did not eradicate the syncretic platforms in Israel, and thus the mental image of Baal and his influence continued along side Yahweh.

The next salient feature of Baalism in the DH occurs in the efforts of Athaliah (Ahab and Jezebel's daughter) to establish herself as ruler of Judah and her Baalistic religion in the Southern Kingdom. The record reports that Athaliah was slain for her treacherous acts (2 Kgs. 11:16). Mattan, the priest of Baal, was then also slain, and the altars and images of Baal were removed from Baal's temple in Judah (2 Kgs. 11:18).[68] The text implies that Baal's influence did not penetrate the south as deeply and as quickly as the north. However, we shall see that Judah also succumbed to the enticements of Baal.

The next chapter that mentions Baal's name in the DH is 2 Kings 17.[69] In this narrative (2 Kgs. 7:6-18) DTR explains that it was the idolatrous worship of Baalism by the children of Israel in the Northern Kingdom that led to their removal by Assyria from the promise land. In 2 Kings 18-20, DTR implies that the acts of Hezekiah, king of Judah have spared the destruction of the remaining Southern Kingdom for a season. 2 Kings 18:3-4 insinuates that Hezekiah was pleasing to Yahweh largely because of his removal of the Baalistic cultic object images from the land.

The literature reveals that Hezekiah's efforts were short-lived, mostly because of the influence of his son Manasseh, who reigned in Judah fifty-five years following his death (2 Kgs. 20:21; 21:1-2). 2 Kings 21:2-4 explains,

> (2) He did evil in the eyes of Yahweh, following after the abominations of the nations, whom Yahweh had removed from before the children of Israel. (3) He rebuilt the high places that his father Hezekiah had destroyed; he erected altars for Baal and made a sacred post, as King Ahab had done; he bowed down to all the host of heaven and worshipped them. (4)

> And he built altars in the house of Yahweh, of which
> Yahweh said, "In Jerusalem I will put my name."

For these atrocities, Manasseh is marked as the most wicked king in Judah. The text indicates that "Manasseh seduced them [Judah] to do greater evil than the nations that Yahweh had destroyed before the children of Israel" (2 Kgs. 21:9). The literature reveals that Yahweh had said through his prophets that Judah's coming destruction was because Manasseh led Judah into serious sin with idols (2 Kgs. 21:11-12).

Before DTR's account of the exile of Judah, a ray of hope shines briefly in the DH. 2 Kings 22-23 recounts the measures of religious reformation carried out by Josiah in connection with the uncovering of the book of the law. The text specifically mentions that Josiah gathered his kingdom together and read to them all of the book of the covenant that was found in Yahweh's temple (2 Kgs. 23:1-2). Josiah then caused the people to enter into a covenant with Yahweh to do all that the covenant of the book specified (2 Kgs. 23:3). He then ordered the removal of the cultic vessels made for Baal and Asherah from the temple of Yahweh; he burned them outside Jerusalem (2 Kgs. 23:4).

DTR applauds Josiah's reforming acts as the text records: "And like him there was no king before him, who turned to Yahweh with all his heart, and with all his soul, according to all the law of Moses; nor did any like him arise after him" (2 Kgs. 23:25). However, with the death of Josiah, reform measures waned. The remainder of the kings of Judah all reigned in wickedness; Judah's corruption, which had reached its zenith in the days of Manasseh, returned. The text suggests that the exile had commenced because of all the sins which Manasseh had committed (2 Kgs. 24:3). Such sins centered in Baalism.

NOTES

1. Cross, *Canaanite Myth and Hebrew Epic,* 278.

2. F. C. Fensham, "A Few Observations on the Polarization Between Yahweh and Baal in I Kings 17–19," *Zeitschrift für die Alttestamentliche Wissenschaft* 92 (1980): 231–32.

3. James R. Battenfield, "YHWH's Refutation of the Baal Myth through the Actions of Elijah and Elisha," in *Israel's Apostasy and Restoration: Essays in Honor of Roland K. Harrison,* ed. Avraham Gileadi (Grand Rapids, Mich.: Baker Book House, 1988), 30.

4. De Boer, review of *The Stories of Elijah and Elisha as Polemics against Baal Worship,* 269.

5. Walter J. Harrelson, "Calf, Golden," in vol. 1 of *The Interpreter's Dictionary of the Bible,* ed. George A. Buttrick, Thomas Samuel Kepler, John Knox, Herbert Gordon May, Samuel Terrein, and Emory Stevens Bucker (Nashville: Abingdon Press, 1982), 488, maintains that the translation of calf is misleading and should be rendered as young bull based on Psalm 106:19–20.

6. See also Exod. 32:4.

7. H. Th. Obbink, "Jahwebilder," *Zeifschrift für die Alttestamentliche Wissenschaft* 47 (1947): 264–74. The pedestal concept is especially treated on p. 264. William F. Albright, *From the Stone Age to Christianity,* 2d ed. (Baltimore: Johns Hopkins, 1957), 299, later concurred with Obbink's theory of the animal being used as a pedestal for Yahweh. He also emphasized that the image of the bull viewed as a representation of Yahweh by most scholars is a gross misconception and must be viewed only as a pedestal for the invisible Yahweh, because the Syro-Palestinian iconography consistently attests that the gods almost always are depicted as standing upon the backs of the animals. Nahum M. Sarna, *Exploring Exodus: The Heritage of Biblical Israel* (New York: Schocken Books, 1986), 218, is also of the opinion that the cultic image was to be used as a pedestal for Yahweh.

8. Obbink, "Jahwebilder," 272.

9. Harrelson, "Calf, Golden," 489.

10. Cross, *Canaanite Myth and Hebrew Epic,* 279.

11. C. F. Burney, *Notes on the Hebrew Text of the Book of Kings* (Oxford: Clarendon Press, 1983), 206, suggests that Ethbaal's name means either "Baal is with him," or implies the idea of Ethbaal being "under Baal's protection."

12. Robert L. Cohn, "The Literary Logic of I Kings 17–19," *Journal of Biblical Literature* 101, pt. 3 (September 1982): 334. See also Russell Inman Gregory, "Elijah's Story Under Scrutiny: A Literary-Critical Analysis of I Kings 17–19" (Ph.D. diss., Vanderbilt University, 1983), 91, who concurs with Cohn.

13. Ibid.

14. Fensham, "A Few Observations of the Polarization Between Yahweh and Baal in I Kings 17–19," 228. For general information regarding the structure of I Kings 17–19, see this entire article on pp. 227–36.

15. Alan J. Hauser, "Yahweh vs. Death—The Real Struggle in I Kings 17–19," *Journal for the Study of the Old Testament,* Supplemental Series, #85, ed. David J. A. Clines and Philip R. Davies (Sheffield: Almond Press, 1990), 81.

16. This quote is taken from the Whiston's translation of *Josephus Complete Works,* 190.

17. Luke 4:25.

18. Burney, *Notes on the Hebrew Text of the Book of Kings,* 222.

19. Otto Eissfeldt, *Der Gott Karmel* (Berlin: Akademie Verlag, 1953), 24.

20. Brown et al., *A Hebrew and English Lexicon of the Old Testament,* 502.

21. Isa. 35:2; Jer. 50:19 and Mic. 7:19. Song of Sol. 7:5.

22. Aharoni, *The Land of the Bible,* 341.

23. Stephen Szikszai, "Elijah the Prophet," in vol. 2 of *The Interpreter's Dictionary of the Bible,* ed. George A. Buttrick, Thomas Samuel Kepler, John Knox, Herbert Gordon May, Samuel Terrein, and Emory Stevens Bucker (Nashville: Abingdon Press, 1982), 89.

24. Gerhard von Rad, *Old Testament Theology, Vol. II: The Theology of Israel's Prophetic Traditions,* trans. D. M. G. Stalker (New York: Harper & Row, 1965), 16.

25. Eakin, "The Relationship between Yahwism and Baalism During the Pre-Exilic Period."

26. Ibid., 17.

27. D. R. Ap-Thomas, "Elijah on Mount Carmel," *Palestine Exploration Quarterly* (January-June 1960): 148.

28. Although I had this idea independent of any other source, later I learned that John Gray, *I & II Kings: A Commentary,* 2d rev. ed. (London: SCM Press, 1970), 393, had arrived at this same conclusion.

29. The altar may have been cut down under the direction of Jezebel, who had also tried to cut off the prophets of Yahweh (1 Kings 18:4).

30. For a discussion of the biblical usage of numbers in general see, Marvin H. Pope, "Number, Numbering, Numbers," in vol. 3 of *The Interpreter's Dictionary of the Bible,* ed. George A. Buttrick, Thomas Samuel Kepler, John Knox, Herbert Gordon May, Samuel Terrein, and Emory Stevens Bucker (Nashville: Abingdon Press, 1982), 561–67. See especially pp. 564–67 for the symbolic usage of numbers in Israel. On p. 564, Pope notes that seven is often used to represent completion; thus three plus four equals seven and may be used together to indicate that the drought is complete. Furthermore, three multiplied by four equals twelve, which may again refer to the twelve tribes. Although admittedly this is mere speculation, the notion that the numbers are to be viewed symbolically cannot be overlooked.

31. Patai, "The 'Control of Rain' in Ancient Palestine," 256.

32. Gregory, "Elijah's Story Under Scrutiny," 123.

33. Brown et al., *A Hebrew and English Lexicon of the Old Testament*, 77; Patai, "The 'Control of Rain' in Ancient Palestine," 256–57; Gray, *I & II Kings*, 385. M. Avi-Yonah, "Mount Carmel and the God of Baalbek," *Israel Exploration Journal* 2 (No. 1, 1952): 124, also maintains that this fire spoken of was really lightning. A. Lucas, "The Miracle on Mount Carmel," *Palestine Exploration Journal* (1945): 49–50; R. H. Kennett, *Old Testament Essays* (Cambridge: Cambridge University Press, 1928), 103–4.

34. The number seven here again seems to represent the concept of completion. For more information regarding the number seven see, Marvin H. Pope, "Seven, Seventh, Seventy," in vol. 4 of *The Interpreter's Dictionary of the Bible*, ed. George A. Buttrick, Thomas Samuel Kepler, John Knox, Herbert Gordon May, Samuel Terrein, and Emory Stevens Bucker (Nashville: Abingdon Press, 1982), 294–95.

35. Nicholas J. Tromp, "Water and Fire on Mount Carmel: A Conciliatory Suggestion," *Biblica* 56 (1975): 494–95.

36. Ibid., 501.

37. The name Elijah, as contrasted here with the name of Jezebel, may also imply a polemical element. The Hebrew name Elijah is translated "my God is Yahweh." On the other hand, Gray, *I & II Kings*, 368 states: "The name Jezebel (*'izebel*) as pointed in MT is an obvious parody. The first perversion of the name may have been *'zebul* ('Where is the Prince?'), then with the scribal perversion of zebul, the title of Baal, to zebel ('dung'). [Z]ebul is known as an element in the divine name Baalzebul, and is now known as one of the stock titles of Baal in the Ras Shamra texts, meaning 'Prince'." Dorothea Ward Harvey, "Jezebel," in vol. 2 of *The Interpreter's Dictionary of the Bible*, ed. George A. Buttrick, Thomas Samuel Kepler, John Knox, Herbert Gordon May, Samuel Terrein, and Emory Stevens Bucker (Nashville: Abingdon Press, 1982), 905 also views this name as a dysphemism.

Yigael Yadin, "The 'House of Ba'al' of Ahab and Jezebel in Samaria, and that of Athalia in Judah," in *Archaeology in the Levant: Essays for Kathleen Kenyon*, ed. Roger Moorey and Peter Parr (Warminster, England: Aris and Phillips, 1978), 128 also points out here that Ahab's children have names which contain Yahwistic theophoric elements: Yehoram, Ahaziahu and Athaliah. Even Ahab's servant that laboured closely by him was named Obadiah, "servant of

Yahweh." This suggests that Ahab did not have near the zeal for Baalism that Jezebel had.

38. The literature portrays Elijah going to Horeb and fasting for forty days as Moses was said to have done (Exod. 24:18). Cross, *Canaanite Myth and Hebrew Epic,* 191, suggests that 1 Kgs. 18–19 is shaped to portray Elijah as a new Moses. Various points of comparison between these two prophets are discussed on pp. 192–93.

39. See also Deut. 33:2 and Judg. 5:4, as well as the discussion of this issue under the heading of *Judges 5* in Chapter 3.

40. Cross, *Canaanite Myth and Hebrew Epic,* 194.

41. A. S. Peake, "Elijah and Jezebel. The Conflict with the Tyrian Baal," *Bulletin of the John Rylands Library* 2 (1927): 319.

42. Cohn, "The Literary Logic of I Kings 17–19," 349–50.

43. Frank E. Eakin, Jr., "Yahweh and Baalism Before the Exile," *Journal of Biblical Literature* 84 (1965): 414.

44. H. H. Rowley, "Elijah on Mount Carmel," *Bulletin of the John Rylands Library* 43 (1960): 219.

45. The text indicates that when Ahab died, the dogs licked up his blood (1 Kgs. 22:38), fulfilling the prophesy of this event as uttered by Elijah in 1 Kgs. 21:37.

46. Battenfield, "YHWH's Refutation of the Baal Myth through the Actions of Elijah and Elisha," 26; Mulder, "Baal in the Old Testament," 194. James A. Montgomery notes that the reading Beelzebul, rather than Beelzebub, occurs in the Chester Beatty papyri for the New Testament references of Matt. 10:25, 12:24; Mark 3:22; Luke 11:15ff (*A Critical and Exegetical Commentary on the Books of Kings,* vol. 10 of *The International Critical Commentary,* ed. Henry Snyder Gehman [New York: Charles Scribner's Sons, 1951], 349).

47. Compare to Job 1:16, where the text reveals that fire from God also consumed not only servants, but also sheep.

48. The idea of lightning being associated with fire is also evidenced in Ezek. 1:13, which states: "and lightning issued from the fire." Brown et al., *A Hebrew and English Lexicon of the Old Testament*, 77, suggest that perhaps lightning rather than fire is intended in this narrative (2 Kgs. 1:10, 12, 14), as well as in the Mount Carmel pericope (1 Kgs. 18:24, 38), where fire descends from Yahweh.

49. See especially Josh. 3:7, 13; 4:14.

50. Mordechai Cogan and Hayim Tadmor, *II Kings*, vol. 11 of *The Anchor Bible*, ed. W. F. Albright and D. N. Freedman (Garden City, N.Y.: Doubleday, 1988), 30–31, translate *seara* as storm rather than whirlwind as most scholars do. They also indicate that this word is sometimes associated with theophany, as in Job 38:1 and Job 40:6.

51. Battenfield, "YHWH's Refutation of the Baal Myth through the Actions of Elijah and Elisha," 27.

52. For the translation of this passage from KTU and my earlier discussion of the parting of the Jordan River, see the subheading *Joshua 2:9–11* in Chapter 3.

53. Cogan and Tadmor, *II Kings*, 37, state: "An unmistakable literary affinity exist between the tale of Moses and that of Elisha; in both, the prophet acts after hearing a complaint and casts (*hslk, cf. Exod. 15:25 and 2 Kgs. 2:21) a healing agent (*rp', cf. Exod. 15:26; 2 Kgs. 2:21, 22) into the bitter source."

54. For a picture depicting Baal with this inherent power of governing the waters, see Pritchard, *The Ancient Near East in Pictures Relating to the Old Testament*, 307, picture no. 490.

55. Leah Bronner, *The Stories of Elijah and Elisha as Polemics Against Baal Worship*, vol. 6 of *Pretoria Oriental Series*, ed. A. Van Selms (Leiden: E. J. Brill, 1968), 55-56.

56. Battenfield, "YHWH's Refutation of the Baal Myth through the Actions of Elijah and Elisha," 27.

57. Ibid., 28.

58. Ibid.

59. See Jared J. Jackson, "Deep, The," in vol. 1 of *The Interpreter's Dictionary of the Bible,* ed. George A. Buttrick, Thomas Samuel Kepler, John Knox, Herbert Gordon May, Samuel Terrein, and Emory Stevens Bucker (Nashville: Abingdon Press, 1982), 813-14, for a discussion of how *tehom* and *tehomot* may be used in the Hebrew Bible.

60. Norman N. Snaith, "The First and Second Books of Kings," in vol. 3 of *The Interpreter's Dictionary of the Bible,* ed. George A. Buttrick, Thomas Samuel Kepler, John Knox, Herbert Gordon May, Samuel Terrein, and Emory Stevens Bucker (Nashville: Abingdon Press, 1982), 213, comments on the idea of Naaman desiring to take earth back to his homeland: "This points to the religious idea of that day that each land had its own god who could be worshipped only there. To leave one land for another was to leave one god for another. Hence, if Naaman was to worship the God of Israel in Syria, he must take some of the soil of Israel with him."

61. Cogan and Tadmor, *II Kings,* 65. These authors also point out that this is the only case in which the cult of Rimmon is attested in the Hebrew Bible. For further information regarding Rimmon, see Jonas C. Greenfield, "The Aramaean God of Rammon/Rimmon," *Israel Exploration Journal* 26 (1976): 195-98.

62. John Gray, "Rimmon," in vol. 4 of *The Interpreter's Dictionary of the Bible,* ed. George A. Buttrick, Thomas Samuel Kepler, John Knox, Herbert Gordon May, Samuel Terrein, and Emory Stevens Bucker (Nashville: Abingdon Press, 1982), 99.

63. John Gray, "Hadadrimmon," in vol. 2 of *The Interpreter's Dictionary of the Bible,* ed. George A. Buttrick, Thomas Samuel Kepler, John Knox, Herbert Gordon May, Samuel Terrein, and Emory Stevens Bucker (Nashville: Abingdon Press, 1982), 507.

64. See 1 Kgs. 17:1.

65. The text later indicates that reprieve from this harsh condition did come, Yahweh caused the sound of chariots to be heard by the Syrian camp, who therefore left their spoils for Israel to seize (2 Kgs. 7:3-16).

66. J. C. De Moor, "The Seasonal Pattern in the Ugaritic Myth of Ba'lu According to the Version of Ilimilku," in vol. 16 of *Alter Orient*

und Altes Testament, ed. Kurt Bergerhof, Manfried Dietrich, and Oswald Loretz (Neukirchen-Vluyn: Butzon & Bercker Kevelaer, 1971), 162-63. The author lists in note #2 on p. 163 the following references where *ᵓarubbot* is attested in the Hebrew Bible: Gen. 7:11; 8:2; 2 Kgs. 7:2, 19; Isa. 24:18; Mal. 3:10.

67. Yadin, "The 'House of Baal' of Ahab and Jezebel in Samaria, and that of Athalia in Judah," 127-29, suggests that this House of Baal was probably located on Mount Carmel.

68. Ibid., 130-32.

69. Baal's name is attested in verse 16, although the entire pericope implies the worship of Baalism.

CONCLUSION

This investigation has demonstrated that DTR launched a literary attack against Baalism, which included the implicit polemical usage of every aspect of water and storm. Several examples were brought from each book of the Deuteronomic corpus in order to reveal DTR's agenda: instructing Israel that Yahwism and not Baalism held the keys to a prosperous life in the land of Canaan. DTR also made certain in the DH that Israel was continually reminded of Yahweh's divine power and of his ability to provide and protect his chosen people on condition of their obedience to the stipulations of the Yahwistic covenant.

DTR clearly demonstrated how Yahweh had warned his people, "Take care not to be lured away to serve other gods and bow to them. For Yahweh's anger will flare up against you, and He will shut up the skies so that there will be no rain and the ground will not yield its produce; and you will soon perish from the good land that Yahweh has assigned to you" (Deut. 11:16-17).

Jeremiah, who was a contemporary of DTR and probably a supporter of the DH,[1] asked this penetrating question when severe droughts occurred in Judah (Jer. 14:1)[2] and the exile drew nigh: "Can any of the false gods of the nations give rain? Can the skies of themselves give showers? Only you are He, O Yahweh our God! Therefore we will wait for you, for you made these things" (Jer 14:22).

However, Judah, like Israel in the north, did not wait upon Yahweh and Yahweh could no longer wait for his people to return. Thus, DTR makes clear that in spite of Yahweh's continual demonstration of power over Baal's supposed domain of water and storm, the south apostatized as well and essentially drowned in Baalism.

This dissertation represents but one portion of the history of the metaphor of water in the Hebrew Bible. There are three major stages to this motif which consist of Yahweh's demonstration of *power*, which includes organization and protection; *promise*, which includes provision through the stipulations of the covenant; and *pedagogy*, the teaching of torah theology.

Although only the final stage is overtly pedagogic, the water motif is a consistent expression of this model throughout the concept of the divine relationship to the development of Israelite culture. As the Hebrew Bible came to a close, the need to launch a literary attack against Baalism or idolatry in general was no longer necessary as the urban movement developed and Judah returned to the Law. What is attested in the Judaic literature after the close of the canon is the issue of torah theology and divine instruction.

The contribution which this study has made has been in the area of stage one of the history of the metaphor of water in the Hebrew Bible. Although this level has been investigated by other scholars, the uniqueness of this study is that it explores the polemical aspects of water language in the Deuteronomic History, especially as it pertains to Baal. I readily admit that this is but one brick in the wall of knowledge in this area, but it is a valid contribution which I hope will aid further studies in understanding this field of research.

NOTES

1. Weinfeld, *Deuteronomy and the Deuteronomic School,* 160.

2. The Book of Jeremiah has more references to drought and famine than any other book in the Hebrew Bible.

SELECTED BIBLIOGRAPHY

Ackerman, James S. "Prophecy and Warfare in Early Israel: A Study of the Deborah-Barak Story." *Bulletin for the American Schools of Oriental Research* (No. 220, 1975): 5–13.

Aharoni, Yohanan. *The Land of the Bible: A Historical Geography*. Rev. ed. Translated and edited by A. F. Rainey. Philadelphia: Westminster Press, 1979.

Albright, William F. *Archaeology and the Religion of Israel*. Baltimore: Johns Hopkins Press, 1942.

————. *The Archaeology of Palestine*. Harmondsworth, Middlesex: Penguin Books, 1951.

————. *From the Stone Age to Christianity*. 2d ed. Baltimore: Johns Hopkins, 1957.

————. "The Old Testament and the Canaanite Language and Literature." *The Catholic Biblical Quarterly* 7 (1945): 5–31.

————. Review of *El in the Ugaritic Texts*, by Marvin J. Pope. *Journal of Biblical Literature* 75 (1956): 255–57.

————. "Some Remarks on the Song of Moses in Deuteronomy XXXII." *Vetus Testamentum* 9 (1959): 339–46.

_____. "The Song of Deborah in the Light of Archaeology." *BASOR* 62 (April 1936): 26–31.

_____. *Yahweh and the Gods of Canaan*. Garden City, N.Y.: Doubleday, 1968.

_____. "Zabul Yamm and Thapit-Nahar in the Combat between Baal and the Sea." *Journal of the Palestine Oriental Society* 16 (1936): 17–20.

Amiet, Pierre. *Ancient Near East*. Translated by John Shepley and Claude Choquet. New York: Harry N. Abrams, Inc., 1980.

Amit, Yairah. "Judges 4: Its Contents and Forms." *Journal for the Study of the Old Testament* 39 (1987): 89–111.

Anderson, A. A. *II Samuel*. Vol. 11 of *Word Biblical Commentary*, edited by David A. Hubbard and Glenn W. Barker. Dallas, Texas: Waco Books, 1989.

Anderson, Bernard W. *Understanding the Old Testament*. Englewood Cliffs, N.J.: Prentice Hall, 1957.

_____. *Understanding the Old Testament*. 3d ed. Englewood Cliffs, N.J.: Prentice-Hall, 1975.

Anderson, George W. *A Critical Introduction to the Old Testament*. London: Gerald Duckworth & Co., 1959.

Ap-Thomas, D. R. "Elijah on Mount Carmel." *Palestine Exploration Quarterly* (January-June 1960): 146–55.

Arayaprateep, Kamol. "A Note on yr' in Jos. IV 24." *Vetus Testamentum* 22 (April 1972): 240–42.

Avi-Yonah, M. "Mount Carmel and the God of Baalbek." *Israel Exploration Journal* 2 (No. 1, 1952): 118–24.

Baldwin, Joyce G. "1 and 2 Samuel: An Introduction and Commentary." In *The Tyndale Old Testament Commentaries*, edited by D. J. Wiseman. Leicester, England: Intervarsity Press, 1988.

Baly, Dennis. *The Geography of the Bible*. New York: Harper & Row, 1957.

————. *The Geography of the Bible*. Rev. ed. New York: Harper & Row, 1974.

————. *God and History in the Old Testament*. New York: Harper & Row, 1976.

Battenfield, James R. "YHWH's Refutation of the Baal Myth through the Actions of Elijah and Elisha." In *Israel's Apostasy and Restoration: Essays in Honor of Roland K. Harrison*, edited by Avraham Gileadi. Grand Rapids, Mich.: Baker Book House, 1988.

Beer, George. *Exodus*. Vol. 3 of *Handbuch zum Alten Testament*, edited by Otto Eissfeldt. Tubingen, Germany: J. C. B. Mohr, 1939.

Bentzen, Aage. *Introduction to the Old Testament*. 2 vols. Copenhagen: G. E. C. Gads, 1949.

Blenkinsopp, J. "Ballad Style and Psalm Style in the Song of Deborah." *Biblica* 42 (1961): 61–76.

Boling, Robert G. *Joshua: A New Translation with Notes and Commentary*. Vol. 6 of *The Anchor Bible*, edited by W. F. Albright and D. N. Freedman. Garden City, N.Y.: Doubleday, 1982.

————. *Judges*. Vol. 6A of *The Anchor Bible*, edited by W. F. Albright and D. N. Freedman. Garden City, N.Y.: Doubleday, 1964.

Bright, John. *A History of Israel.* 3d ed. Philadelphia: Westminster Press, 1981.

Bronner, Leah. *The Stories of Elijah and Elisha as Polemics Against Baal Worship.* Vol. 6 of *Pretoria Oriental Series*, edited by A. Van Selms. Leiden: E. J. Brill, 1968.

Brooks, Beatrice A. "Fertility Cult Functionaries in the Old Testament." *Journal of Biblical Literature* 60 (1941): 227–53.

Brown, Francis, S. R. Driver, and C. A. Briggs. *A Hebrew and English Lexicon of the Old Testament.* Oxford: Clarendon Press, 1951.

Brueggemann, Walter. "First and Second Samuel." In *Interpretation: A Bible Commentary for Teaching and Preaching*, edited by James Luther Mays, Patrick D. Miller, Jr., and Paul J. Achtemeier. Louisville, Ky.: John Knox Press, 1990.

————. *The Land. Place as Gift, Promise and Challenge in Biblical Faith.* Philadelphia: Fortress Press, 1977.

Burney, C. F. *The Book of Judges with an Introduction and Notes on the Hebrew Text of the Book of Kings with an Introduction and Appendix.* New York: KTAV Publishing House, 1970.

————. *Notes on the Hebrew Text of the Book of Kings.* Oxford: Clarendon Press, 1983.

Burroughs, Millar. "Syncretism in the Old Testament." *The Journal of Bible and Religion* 9 (1941): 10–16.

Butler, Trent C. *Joshua.* Vol. 7 of *Word Biblical Commentary*, edited by David A. Hubbard and Glenn W. Barker. Waco, Tex.: Word Books Publisher, 1982.

Caquot, Andre, and Maurice Sznycer. *Ugaritic Religion.* Leiden: E. J. Brill, 1980.

Carlson, R. A. "Elie A L'Horeb." *Vetus Testamentum* 19 (1969): 416–39.

Cassuto, M. D. *From Adam to Noah.* 2d ed. N.p., 1953.

Cassuto, Umberto. "Baal and Mot in the Ugaritic Texts." *Israel Exploration Journal* 12 (1962): 77–86.

_____. *The Goddess Anath. Canaanite Epics of the Patriarchal Age.* Translated by Israel Abrahams. Jerusalem: The Magnes Press, The Hebrew University, 1971.

Childs, Brevard S. *Introduction to the Old Testament As Scripture.* Philadelphia: Fortress Press, 1979.

Chisholm, Robert Bruce. "An Exegetical and Theological Study of Psalm 18 / 2 Samuel 22." Ph.D. diss., Dallas Theological Seminary, 1983.

Clements, R. E. "Deuteronomy." In *Old Testament Guides,* edited by R. N. Whybray. Sheffield: JSOT Press, 1989.

_____. *Deuteronomy.* Sheffield: Academic Press, 1989.

_____. "Deuteronomy and the Jerusalem Cult Tradition." *Vetus Testamentum* 15 (1965): 300–312.

Clifford, Richard. "Deuteronomy with an Excursus on Covenant and Law." In Vol. 4 of *Old Testament Message: A Biblical Theologial Commentary,* edited by C. Stuhlmueller, C. P. McNamara and M. McNamara. Wilmington, Del.: Michael Glazier, 1982.

Cogan, Michael David, ed. and trans. *Stories from Ancient Canaan.* Philadelphia: Westminster Press, 1978.

Cogan, Mordechai, and Hayim Tadmor. *II Kings: A New Translation with Introduction and Commentary.* Vol. 11 of *The Anchor Bible,* edited by W. F. Albright and D. N. Freedman. Garden City, N.Y.: Doubleday, 1984.

Cohn, Robert L. "The Literary Logic of I Kings 17–19." *Journal of Biblical Literature* 101, pt. 3 (September 1982): 333–50.

Covensky, Milton. *The Ancient Near East Tradition.* New York: Harper & Row, 1966.

Craigie, Peter C. "The Book of Deuteronomy." In *The New International Commentary in the Old Testament*, edited by R. K. Harrison. Grand Rapids, Mich: William B. Eerdsman Publishing Co., 1976.

_____. "Some Further Notes on the Song of Deborah." *Vetus Testamentum* 22 (July 1972): 349–53.

Crenshaw, James. *Prophetic Conflict: Its Effect upon Israelite Religion.* Berlin: Walter de Gruyter, 1971.

Cross, Frank Moore. *Canaanite Myth and Hebrew Epic.* Cambridge: Harvard University Press, 1973.

_____. "'The Divine Warrior' in Israel's Early Cult." In *Biblical Motifs: Origins and Transformations*, edited by Alexander Altmann. Cambridge: Harvard University Press, 1963.

Cross, Frank Moore, and David Noel Freedman. "The Blessing of Moses." *Journal of Biblical Literature* 67 (1948): 191–210.

_____. "A Note on Deuteronomy 33:26." *Bulletin of the American School of Oriental Research* (December 1947): 6–7.

_____. "A Royal Song of Thanksgiving: II Samuel-Psalms 18." *Journal of Biblical Literature* 72 (1953): 15–34.

_____. "The Song of Miriam." *Journal of Near Eastern Studies* 14 (January-October 1955): 237–50.

_____. *Studies in Ancient Yahwistic Poetry.* Missoula, Mont.: Scholars Press, 1975.

Curtis, A. H. W. "The 'Subjugation of the Water' Motif in the Psalms: Imagery or Polemic?" *Journal of Semitic Studies* 23 (Autumn 1978): 245–56.

Dahood, Mitchell A. "Ancient Semitic Deities in Syria and Palestine." In *Le Antiche Divinita Semitiche,* edited by Sabatino Moscati. In *Studi Semitici* 1 (Centro di Studi Semitici, 1958).

_____. *Psalms I: 1–50.* Vol. 16 of *The Anchor Bible,* edited by W. F. Albright and D. N. Freedman. Garden City, N.Y.: Doubleday, 1965–66.

Day, John. "Asherah in the Hebrew Bible and Northwest Semitic Literature." *Journal of Biblical Literature* 105 (September 1986): 385–408.

_____. *God's Conflict with the Dragon and the Sea: Echoes of a Canaanite Myth in the Old Testament.* Cambridge: Cambridge University Press, 1985.

_____. "The Old Testament Utilization of Language and Imagery Having Parallels in the Baal Mythology of the Ugaritic Texts." Ph.D. diss., University of Cambridge, 1973.

De Boer, P. A. H. Review of *The Stories of Elijah and Elisha as Polemics against Baal Worship,* by Leah Bronner. *Vetus Testamentum* 19 (1969): 267–69.

De Moor, J. C. " 'ar 'Honey Dew.'" *Ugarit-Forschungen* 7 (1975): 590–91.

_____. "'asherah." In Vol. 2 of *Theological Dictionary of the Old Testament,* edited by G. Johannes Botterweck and Helmer Ringgren, translated by John T. Willis. Grand Rapids, Mich.: William B. Eerdsman Publishing Co., 1986.

_____. "ba'al." In Vol. 2 of *Theological Dictionary of the Old Testament*, edited by G. Johannes Botterweck and Helmer Ringgren, translated by John T. Willis. Grand Rapids, Mich.: William B. Eerdsman Publishing Co., 1986.

_____. "The Seasonal Pattern in the Ugaritic Myth of Ba'lu According to the Version of Ilimilku." In Vol. 16 of *Alter Orient und Altes Testament*, edited by Kurt Bergerhof, Manfried Dietrich, and Oswald Loretz, 127–35. Neukirchen-Vluyn: Butzon & Bercker Kevelaer, 1971.

de Vaux, Roland. *Ancient Israel. Its Life and Institutions*. Translated by John McHugh. New York: McGraw-Hill, 1961.

De Vries, Simon J. "Temporal Terms As Structural Elements in the Holy War Tradition." *Vetus Testamentum* 25 (January 1975): 80–105.

Dietrich, M., O. Loretz, and J. Sanmartin, with H. W. Kisker. *Die keilalphabetischen Texte aus Ugarit. Einschliesslich der Keilaphabetischen Texte ausserhalb Ugarit. 1. Transkription.* Alter Orient und Altes Testament 24. Kevelaer and Neukirchen-Vluyn: Verlag Butzon und Bercker and Neukirchen Verlag, 1976.

Dietrich, Walter. *Prophetie und Geschichte: eine redaktionsgeschichtliche Untersuchung zum Deuteronomistischen Geschichteswerk* Heft 108 of *Forschungen zur Religion und Literatur des Alten und Neuen Testaments*, Gottingen: Vandenhoeck & Ruprecht, 1972.

Driver, G. R. *Canaanite Myths and Legends.* Edinburgh: T & T Clark, 1956.

Driver, S. R. *A Critical and Exegetical Commentary on Deuteronomy.* Vol. 5 of *The International Critical Commentary*, edited by S. R. Driver, Alfred Plummer, and Charles A. Briggs. New York: Charles Scribner's Sons, 1895.

————. *An Introduction to the Literature of the Old Testament.* Cleveland: Meridian Books, 1967.

————. *Notes on the Hebrew Text and Topography of the Books of Samuel.* 2d ed. Oxford: Clarendon Press, 1913.

Eakin, Frank E., Jr. "The Reed Sea and Baalism." *Journal of Biblical Literature* 86, pt. 4 (December 1967): 378–84.

————. "The Relationship between Yahwism and Baalism During the Pre-Exilic Period." Ph.D. diss., Duke University, 1964.

————. *The Religion and Culture of Israel: An Introduction to Old Testament Thought.* Boston: Allyn and Bacon, 1971.

————. "Yahweh and Baalism Before the Exile." *Journal of Biblical Literature* 84 (1965): 407–414.

Eissfeldt, Otto. "Ba'alsamen und Jahwe." *Zeitschrift für die alttestamentliche Wissenschaft* 57 (1939): 1–31.

————. *Baal Zephon, Zeus Kasios und der Durchzug der Israeliten durchs Meer.* Halle: Max Niemeyer Verlag, 1932.

————. *Der Gott Karmel.* Berlin: Akademie Verlag, 1953.

————. *The Old Testament: An Introduction.* Translated by Peter R. Ackroyd. New York: Harper & Row, 1965.

Emerton, J. A. "Gideon and Jerubbaal." *Journal of Theological Studies* 27, pt. 2 (1976): 289–312.

Even-Shoshan, Abraham. *A New Concordance of the Old Testament Using the Hebrew and Aramaic Text.* Jerusalem: Kiryat Sepher, 1985.

Fensham, F. C. "The Burning of the Golden Calf and Ugarit." *Israel Exploration Journal* 16 (1966): 191–93.

_____. "A Few Observations on the Polarization Between Yahweh and Baal in I Kings 17–19." *Zeitschrift für die Alttestamentliche Wissenschaft* 92 (1980): 227–36.

_____. "Thunder-stones in Ugarit." *Journal of Near Eastern Studies* 18 (1959): 273–74.

Fohrer, Georg. *Introduction to the Old Testament.* 10th ed. Translated by David E. Green. Nashville: Abingdon Press, 1968.

Forsyth, Neil. *The Old Enemy: Satan and the Combat Myth.* Princeton, N.J.: Princeton University Press, 1987.

Frankfort, H., and H. A. Frankfort. *The Intellectual Adventure of Ancient Man.* Chicago: University of Chicago Press, 1946.

Freedman, David Noel. "The Deuteronomic History." In Supplementary Volume of *The Interpreter's Dictionary of the Bible*, edited by George A. Buttrick, Thomas Samuel Kepler, John Knox, Herbert Gordon May, Samuel Terrein, and Emory Stevens Bucker, 226–28. Nashville: Abingdon Press, 1982.

_____. "Early Israelite History in the Light of the Early Israelite Poetry." In *Unity and Diversity: Essays in the History, Literature and Religion of the Ancient Near East*, edited by H. Goedicke and J. J. M. Roberts. Baltimore: Johns Hopkins University Press, 1975.

_____. "Pentateuch." In Vol. 3 of *The Interpreter's Dictionary of the Bible*, edited by George A. Buttrick, Thomas Samuel Kepler, John Knox, Herbert Gordon May, Samuel Terrein, and Emory Stevens Bucker, 711–27. Nashville: Abingdon Press, 1982.

_____. "Who Is Like Thee Among The Gods?" In *Ancient Israelite Religion: Essays in Honor of Frank Moore Cross*, edited by Patrick D. Miller, Jr., Paul D. Hanson, and S. Dean McBride. Philadelphia: Fortress Press, 1987.

Fretheim, Terrance E. "Deuteronomic History." In *Interpreting Biblical Texts*, edited by Lloyd Bailey, Sr., and Victor P. Furnish. Nashville: Abingdon Press, 1983.

Friedman, Richard Elliot. *Who Wrote the Bible?* New York: Harper & Row, 1989.

Gaster, Theodore H. *Thespis: Ritual, Myth, and Drama in the Ancient Near East*. Rev. ed. New York: Gordian Press, 1975.

Gerhardt, Walter, Jr. "The Weather-God in the Ancient Near Eastern Literature with Special Reference to Hebrew Bible." Ph.D. diss., The Dropsie College for Hebrew and Cognate Learning, 1963.

Gibson, J. C. L. "The Theology of the Ugaritic Baal Cycle." *Orientalia* 53 (1984): 202–19.

Globe, Alexander. "The Literary Structure and Unity of the Song of Deborah." *Journal of Biblical Literature* 93 (December 1974): 493–512.

Glueck, Nelson. *The Jordan River*. Philadelphia: Westminster Press, 1946.

Gordon, Cyrus H. "Canaanite Mythology." In *Mythologies of the Ancient World*, edited by Samuel Noah Kramer, 181–218. Garden City, N.Y.: Doubleday, 1961.

_____. "Sabbatical Cycle or Seasonal Pattern." *Orientalia* 22 (1953): 79–81.

_____. *Ugaritic Handbook*. Rome: Pontificium Institutum Biblicum, 1947.

_____. *Ugaritic Literature: A Comprehensive Translation of the Poetic and Prose Texts*. Rome: Pontificium Institutum Biblicum, 1949.

Gordon, Robert P. *I & II Samuel: A Commentary*. Exeter: Paternoster Press, 1986.

Gottwald, Norman K. "War, Holy." In Supplementary Volume of *The Interpreter's Dictionary of the Bible*, edited by George A. Buttrick, Thomas Samuel Kepler, John Knox, Herbert Gordon May, Samuel Terrein, and Emory Stevens Bucker, 942–44. Nashville: Abingdon Press, 1982.

Gray, John. "Ashtoreth." In Vol. 1 of *The Interpreter's Dictionary of the Bible*, edited by George A. Buttrick, Thomas Samuel Kepler, John Knox, Herbert Gordon May, Samuel Terrein, and Emory Stevens Bucker. Nashville: Abingdon Press, 1982.

————. "Baal (Deity)." In Vol. 1 of *The Interpreter's Dictionary of the Bible*, edited by George A. Buttrick, Thomas Samuel Kepler, John Knox, Herbert Gordon May, Samuel Terrein, and Emory Stevens Bucker. Nashville: Abingdon Press, 1982.

————. *I & II Kings: A Commentary*. 2d rev. ed. London: SCM Press, 1970.

————. "Hadadrimmon." In Vol. 2 of *The Interpreter's Dictionary of the Bible*, edited by George A. Buttrick, Thomas Samuel Kepler, John Knox, Herbert Gordon May, Samuel Terrein, and Emory Stevens Bucker. Nashville: Abingdon Press, 1982.

————. "Israel in the Song of Deborah." In *Ascribe to the Lord: Biblical & Other Studies in Memory of Peter C. Craigie*, edited by Lyle Eslinger and Glen Taylor. Sheffield: JSOT Press, 1988.

————. "The Legacy of Canaan. The Ras Shamra Texts and Their Relevance to the Old Testament." In Vol. 5 of *Supplements to Vetus Testamentum*, edited by G. W. Anderson, P. A. H. De Boer, Millar Burrows, Henri Cazelles, E. Hammershaimb, and Martin Noth. Leiden: E. J. Brill, 1957.

————. "Rimmon." In Vol. 4 of *The Interpreter's Dictionary of the Bible*, edited by George A. Buttrick, Thomas Samuel Kepler, John Knox, Herbert Gordon May, Samuel Terrein, and Emory Stevens Bucker. Nashville: Abingdon Press, 1982.

————. "Some Aspects of Canaanite Religion." *Vetus Testamentum* 15 (1966): 170–92.

Gray, John, ed. "Joshua, Judges and Ruth," In *The Century Bible*. New edition. London: Thomas Nelson, Ltd., 1967.

Greenfield, Jonas C. "The Aramaean God of Rammon/Rimmon." *Israel Exploration Journal* 26 (1976): 195–98.

————. "Philistines." In Vol. 3 of *The Interpreter's Dictionary of the Bible*, edited by George A. Buttrick, Thomas Samuel Kepler, John Knox, Herbert Gordon May, Samuel Terrein, and Emory Stevens Bucker. Nashville: Abingdon Press, 1982.

Greenspahn, Frederic E. "The Theology of the Framework of Judges." *Vetus Testamentum* 36 (1986): 385–96.

Greenstein, Edward L. "The Snaring of the Sea in the Baal Epic." *Journal for the Study of the Northwest Semitic Languages and Literatures* 3 (October 1982): 195–216.

Gregory, Russell Inman. "Elijah's Story Under Scrutiny: A Literary-Critical Analysis of I Kings 17–19." Ph.D. diss., Vanderbilt University, 1983.

Guthrie, Harvey H., Jr. "Hadad." In Vol. 2 of *The Interpreter's Dictionary of the Bible*, edited by George A. Buttrick, Thomas Samuel Kepler, John Knox, Herbert Gordon May, Samuel Terrein, and Emory Stevens Bucker. Nashville: Abingdon Press, 1982.

Habel, Norman C. *Yahweh versus Baal: A Conflict of Religious Cultures*. New York: Bookman Associates, 1964.

Haddad, Hassan S. "Baal-Hadad: A Study of the Syrian Storm-God." Ph.D. diss., University of Chicago, 1960.

Halpern, Baruch. *The First Historians: The Hebrew Bible and History*. San Francisco: Harper & Row, 1988.

Harper's Bible Dictionary. Edited by Paul J. Achtemeir, Roger S. Borass, Michael Fishbane, Pheme Perkins, William O. Walker, Jr. San Francisco: Harper & Row, 1985.

Harrelson, Walter J. "Calf, Golden." In Vol. 1 of *The Interpreter's Dictionary of the Bible*, edited by George A. Buttrick, Thomas Samuel Kepler, John Knox, Herbert Gordon May, Samuel Terrein, and Emory Stevens Bucker. Nashville: Abingdon Press, 1982.

Harvey, Dorothea Ward. "Jezebel." In Vol. 2 of *The Interpreter's Dictionary of the Bible*, edited by George A. Buttrick, Thomas Samuel Kepler, John Knox, Herbert Gordon May, Samuel Terrein, and Emory Stevens Bucker. Nashville: Abingdon Press, 1982.

Hauser, Alan J. "Yahweh vs. Death—The Real Struggle in I Kings 17–19." *Journal for the Study of the Old Testament*, Supplemental Series, #85, edited by David J. A. Clines and Philip R. Davies. Sheffield: Almond Press, 1990.

Helck, Wolfgang. *Die Beziehungen Ägyptens zu Vorderasien im 3. und 2. Jahrtausend V. Chr.* Band 5 *Agyptologisch Abhandlungen*, herausgeben von Wolfgang Helck und Eberhard Otto. Wiesbaden: Otto Harrassowitz, 1971.

Hertzberg, Hans Wilhelm. *I & II Samuel: A Commentary*. Translated by J. S. Bowden. Philadelphia: Westminster Press, 1964.

Hoffner, H. A. "Hets." In Vol. 5 of *Theological Dictionary of the Old Testament*, edited by G. Johannes Botterweck and Helmer

Ringgren, translated by David E. Green. Grand Rapids, Mich.: William B. Eerdsman Publishing Co., 1986.

Hvidberg, Flemming F. *Weeping and Laughter in the Old Testament: A Study of Canaanite-Israelite Religion.* Leiden: E. J. Brill, 1962.

Hyatt, J. Philip. "Canaanite Religion and Its Influence in the Hebrews." *Biblical Archaeologist* 2 (February 1939): 6–8.

————. "Jeremiah and Deuteronomy." *Journal of Near Eastern Studies* 1 (1942): 156–73.

Issar, Arie S. *Water Shall Flow from the Rock: Hydrogeology and Climate in the Lands of the Bible.* Berlin: Springer Verlag, 1990.

Jack, J. W. *The Ras Shamra Tablets: Their Bearing on the Old Testament.* Edinburgh: T & T Clark, 1938.

Jackson, Jared J. "Deep, The." In Vol. 1 of *The Interpreter's Dictionary of the Bible,* edited by George A. Buttrick, Thomas Samuel Kepler, John Knox, Herbert Gordon May, Samuel Terrein, and Emory Stevens Bucker. Nashville: Abingdon Press, 1982.

Jeremias, Jöng. *Theophenie. Die Geschicte einer Alttestamentliche Gattung.* Wissenschaftliche Monographien zum Alten und Neven Testament, 10. Neukirchen-Vluyn: Neukirchener Verlag, 1965.

Jobling, William Jeffree. "Canaan, Ugarit and the Old Testament: A Study in Relationships." Ph.D. diss., University of Sydney (Australia), 1976.

Jones, Gwilym H. "'Holy War' or 'Yahweh War?'" *Vetus Testamentum* 25 (1975): 643–58.

Kaiser, O. *Die mythische Bedeuntung des Meeres in Aegypten, Ras Schamra und Israel.* Dactylogramme, Tübungen, 1956.

Kaiser, Walter C., Jr. "The Ugaritic Pantheon." Ph.D. diss., Brandeis University, 1973.

Kapelrud, Arvid S. *Baal in the Ras Shamra Texts.* Copenhagen: G. E. C. Gad Publisher, 1952.

_____. *The Ras Shamra Discoveries and the Old Testament.* Translated by G. W. Anderson. Norman: University of Oklahoma Press, 1963.

_____. "Ugarit." In Vol. 4 of *The Interpreter's Dictionary of the Bible*, edited by George A. Buttrick, Thomas Samuel Kepler, John Knox, Herbert Gordon May, Samuel Terrein, and Emory Stevens Bucker. Nashville: Abingdon Press, 1982.

_____. *The Violent Goddess Anat in the Ras Shamra Texts.* Oslo: Universitetsforlaget, 1969.

Kaufmann, Yehezkel. *The Religion of Israel: From Its Beginnings to the Babylonian Exile.* Translated by Moshe Greenberg. New York: Schocken Books, 1972.

Kees, Hermann. *Ancient Egypt: A Cultural Topography.* Chicago: University of Chicago Press, 1961.

Keil, C. F., and F. Delitzsch. *Joshua, Judges and Ruth.* Vol. 4 of *Biblical Commentary on the Old Testament*, translated by James Martin. Grand Rapids, Mich: William B. Eerdsman Publishing Co., 1950.

Kennett, R. H. *Old Testament Essays.* Cambridge: Cambridge University Press, 1928.

Klein, Lillian R. *The Triumph of Irony in the Book of Judges.* Sheffield: Academic Press, 1988.

Klein, Ralph W. "I Samuel." In Vol. 10 of *Word Biblical Commentary*, edited by David A. Hubbard and Glenn W. Barker. Waco, Tex.: Word Books Publisher, 1982.

Kline, Meredith G. *Treaty of the Great King: The Covenant Structure of Deuteronomy: Studies and Commentary*. Grand Rapids, Mich.: William B. Eerdsman Publishing Co., 1963.

Kloos, Carola. *Yhwh's Combat with the Sea: A Canaanite Tradition in the Religion of Ancient Israel*. Amsterdam: G. A. van Oorschot; Leiden: E. J. Brill, 1986.

Knight, Douglas A., and Gene M. Tucker, eds. *The Hebrew Bible and Its Modern Interpreters*. Philadelphia: Fortress Press; and Chico, Calif.: Scholars Press, 1985.

Kraus, Hans-Joachim. *Psalms 1–59: A Commentary*. Translated by Hilton C. Oswald. Minneapolis: Augsburg Publishing House, 1988.

Labuschagne, C. J. *The Incomparability of Yahweh in the Old Testament*. Vol. 5 of *Pretoria Oriental Series*, edited by A. Van Selms. Leiden: E. J. Brill, 1966.

————. "The Song of Moses: Its Framework and Structure." In *De Fructu Oris Sui: Essays in Honour of Adrianus Van Selms*, edited by I. H. Eybers, F. C. Fensham, C. J. Labuschagne, W. C. Van Wyk, and A. H. Van Zyl, vol. 9 of *Pretoria Oriental Series*, edited by A. Van Selms, 89–98.

Lambert, W. G. "A New Look at the Babylonian Background of Genesis." *Journal of Theological Studies* 16 (1965): 295.

Lasor, William Sanford, David Allan Hubbard, and Frederic William Bush. *Old Testament Survey: The Message, Form, and Background of the Old Testament*. Grand Rapids, Mich.: William B. Eerdsman Publishing Co., 1982.

L'Heurex, Conrad E. *Rank Among The Canaanite Gods El, Ba'al, and the Repha'im*. Harvard Semitic Monographs #21, edited by Frank Moore Cross, Jr. Missoula, Mont.: Scholars Press, 1979.

Lind, Millard C. *Yahweh Is a Warrior: The Theology of Warfare in Ancient Israel*. Scottdale, Penn.: Herald Press, 1980.

Loewenstamm, Samuel E. "The Killing of Mot in Ugaritic Myth." *Orientalia* 41 (1972): 378–82.

Lohfink, Norbert. "The Cult Reform of Josiah of Judah: 2 Kings 22–23 as a Source for the History of Israelite Religion". In *Ancient Israelite Religion: Essays in Honor of Frank Moore Cross*, pp. 459–475, edited by Patrick D. Miller, Jr., Paul D. Hanson, and S. Dean McBride. Philadelphia: Fortress Press, 1987.

————. "Deuteronomy." In Supplementary Volume of *The Interpreter's Dictionary of the Bible*, edited by George A. Buttrick, Thomas Samuel Kepler, John Knox, Herbert Gordon May, Samuel Terrein, and Emory Stevens Bucker. Nashville: Abingdon Press, 1982.

Lohfink, Norbert, ed. *Das Deuteronomium Entstehung Gestalt Und Botschaft*. Belgium: Leuven University Press, 1985.

Long, Burke O. "I Kings with an Introduction to Historical Literature." Vol. 9 of *The Forms of the Old Testament Literature*, edited by Rolf Knierim and Gene M. Tucker. Grand Rapids, Mich.: William B. Eerdsman Publishing Co., 1984.

Longman, Tremper, III. "I Sam 12:16–19: Divine Omnipotence or Covenant Curse?" *Westminster Theological Journal* 45 (No. 1, 1983): 168–71.

Lucas, A. "The Miracle on Mount Carmel." *Palestine Exploration Journal* (1945): 49–50.

Luckenbill, D. *Ancient Records of Assyria and Babylonia.* 2 vols. Chicago, 1926–27.

Lundbom, Jack R. "The Lawbook in the Josianic Reform." *Catholic Biblical Quarterly* 38 (1976): 293–302.

Margalit, Baruch. "A Matter of >Life< and >Death<: A Study of the Baal-Mot Epic (CTA 4–5–6)." In *Alter Orient und Altes Testament. Veroffentlichungen zur Kultur und Geschichte des Alten Orients und des Alten Testaments.* Herausgeben Kurt Bergerhoff, Manfried Dietrich, and Oswald Loretz, Band. 206, Verlag Butzon & Bercker Kevelaer, Neukirchen Verlag: Neukirchen-Vluyn, 1980.

May, Herbert. "Some Cosmic Connotations of Mayim Rabbim, 'Many Waters?'" *Journal of Biblical Literature* 74, pt. 1 (March 1955): 9–21.

Mayes, A. D. H. "Deuteronomy." In *New Century Bible Commentary*, edited by R. E. Clements and Matthew Black. Grand Rapids, Mich.: William B. Eerdsman Publishing Co., 1981.

————. *The Story of Israel Between Settlement and Exile: A Redactional Study of the Deuteronomistic History.* London: SCM Press, 1983.

McCarter, P. Kyle, Jr. *I Samuel: A New Translation with Introduction, Notes & Commentary.* Vol. 8 of *The Anchor Bible*, edited by W. F. Albright and D. N. Freedman. Garden City, N.Y.: Doubleday, 1980.

————. *II Samuel: A New Translation with Introduction, Notes and Commentary.* Vol. 9 of *The Anchor Bible*, edited by W. F. Albright and D. N. Freedman. Garden City, N.Y.: Doubleday, 1984.

McCarthy, Dennis J. "Some Holy War Vocabulary in Joshua 2." *Catholic Biblical Quarterly* 33 (April 1971): 228–30.

————. *Treaty and Covenant: A Study in Form in the Ancient Oriental Documents and in the Old Testament*. Rome: Biblical Institute Press, 1978.

McCown, Chester C. "Cistern." In Vol. 1 of *The Interpreter's Dictionary of the Bible*, edited by George A. Buttrick, Thomas Samuel Kepler, John Knox, Herbert Gordon May, Samuel Terrein, and Emory Stevens Bucker. Nashville: Abingdon Press, 1982.

Meek, Theophile James. *Hebrew Origins*. Rev. ed. New York: Harper & Row, 1950.

Meier, Sam. "Baal's Fight with Yam (KTU 1.2.I,IV). A Part of the Baal Myth as Known in KTU 1.1,3–6?" *Ugarit-Forschungen* 18 (1986): 241–54.

Mendenhall, George E. "Ancient Oriental and Biblical Law." *Biblical Archaeologist* 17 (May 1954): 26–46.

————. "Covenant Forms in Israelite Tradition." *Biblical Archaeologist* 17 (September 1954): 50–76.

————. "The Suzerainty Treaty Structure: Thirty Years Later." In *Religion and Law: Biblical-Judaic Law and Islamic Perspectives*, edited by Edwin B. Firmage, Bernard G. Weiss, and John W. Welch. Winona Lake, Ind.: Eisenbrauns, 1990.

Miller, Patrick D. "Deuteronomy." In *Interpretation: A Bible Commentary for Teaching and Preaching*, edited by James Luther Mays, Patrick D. Miller, Jr., and Paul J. Achtemeier. Louisville, Ky.: John Knox Press, 1990.

————. *The Divine Warrior in Early Israel*. Cambridge: Harvard University Press, 1973.

Montgomery, James A. *A Critical and Exegetical Commentary on the Books of Kings*. Vol. 10 of *The International Critical Commen-*

tary, edited by Henry Snyder Gehman. New York: Charles Scribner's Sons, 1951.

Moore, George Foot. *A Critical Exegetical Commentary on Judges.* Vol. 7 of *The International Critical Commentary*, edited by S. R. Driver, Alfred Plummer, and Charles A. Briggs. New York: Charles Schribner's Sons, 1895.

Moran, W. L. "Some Remarks on the Song of Moses." *Biblica* 43 (1982): 317–27.

————. "A Study of the Deuteronomistic History." *Biblica* 46 (1965): 222–28.

Morenz, Siegfried. *Egyptian Religion.* Translated by Ann E. Keep. Ithaca, N.Y.: Cornell University Press, 1973.

Moscati, Sabatino. *The Face of the Ancient Orient.* Garden City, N.Y.: Doubleday, 1962.

Mulder, M. J. "Baal in the Old Testament." In Vol. 2 of *Theological Dictionary of the Old Testament*, edited by G. Johannes Botterweck and Helmer Ringgren, translated by John T. Willis. Grand Rapids, Mich.: William B. Eerdsman Publishing Co., 1986.

————. "Yesurun." In Vol. 6 of *Theological Dictionary of the Old Testament*, edited by G. Johannes Botterweck and Helmer Ringgren, translated by David E. Green, 472–77. Grand Rapids, Mich.: William B. Eerdsman Publishing Co., 1990.

Mullen, E. Theodore, Jr. *The Divine Council in Canaanite and Early Hebrew Literature.* Harvard Semitic Monographs #24, edited by Frank Moore Cross, Jr. Missoula, Mont.: Scholars Press, 1980.

Murray, D. F. "Narrative Structure and Technique in the Deborah-Barak Story (Judges IV 4–22)." In *Studies in the Historical Books of the Old Testament*, in *Supplements to Vetus Testamentum*, edited by G. W. Anderson, P. A. H. De Boer, Millar

Burrows, Henri Cazelles, E. Hammershaimb, and Martin Noth, 155–89. Leiden: E. J. Brill, 1979.

Nelson, Richard D. *The Double Redaction of the Deuteronomistic History*. Journal for the Study of the Old Testament Supplement Series #18. Sheffield: JSOT Press, 1981.

Nicholson, E. W. *Deuteronomy and Tradition*. Philadelphia: Fortress Press, 1967.

―――. *Preaching to the Exiles: A Study of the Prose Tradition in the Book of Jeremiah*. Oxford: Basil Blackwell, 1970.

North, Christopher R. *The Old Testament Interpretation*. London: Epworth Press, 1953.

Noth, Martin. "The Deuteronomic History." In *Journal for the Study of the Old Testament*, Supplemental Series 15, edited by D. J. A. Clines, P. R. Davies, and D. M. Gunn. Sheffield: JSOT Press. 1981.

―――. *A History of Pentateuchal Traditions*. Translated with an introduction by Bernard W. Anderson. Chico, Calif.: Scholars Press, 1981.

Obbink, H. Th. "Jahwebilder." *Zeifschrift für die Alttestamentliche Wissenschaft* 47 (1947): 264–74.

Obermann, Julian. *Ugaritic Mythology: A Study of Its Leading Motifs*. New Haven, Conn. Yale University Press, 1948.

O'Brien, Mark. *The Deuteronomistic History Hypothesis: A Reassessment*. Fribourg: Editions Universitaires, 1989.

Old Testament Thought. Boston: Allyn and Bacon, 1971.

Oldenburg, Ulf. *The Conflict Between El and Ba'al in Canaanite Religion*. Leiden: E. J. Brill, 1969.

Orni, Efraim, and Elisha Efrat. *Geography of Israel*. 3d rev. ed. Jerusalem: Keter Publishing House, 1971.

Ostborn, Gunnar. *Yahweh and Baal: Studies in the Book of Hosea and Related Documents*. Lund: C. W. K. Gleerup, 1955.

Patai, Raphael. "The 'Control of Rain' in Ancient Palestine: A Study in Comparative Religion." *Hebrew Union College Annual* 14 (1939): 251–86.

————. *The Hebrew Goddess*. 3d ed. Detroit: Wayne State University Press, 1990.

Patton, John Hastings. *Canaanite Parallels in the Book of Psalms*. Baltimore: Johns Hopkins Press, 1944.

Payne, David F. *Deuteronomy*. Philadelphia: The Westminster Press, 1985.

Peake, A. S. "Elijah and Jezebel. The Conflict with the Tyrian Baal." *Bulletin of the John Rylands Library* 2 (1927): 296–319.

Peckham, Brian. "The Composition of the Deuteronomistic History." Number 35 of *Harvard Semitic Monographs*, edited by Frank Moore Cross. Atlanta: Scholars Press, 1985.

Perdue, Leo G., and Brian W. Kovacs, eds. *A Prophet to the Nations: Essays in Jeremiah Studies*. Winona Lake, Ind.: Eisenbrauns, 1984.

Perleman, Alice Lenone. "Asherah and Astarte in the Old Testament and Ugaritic Literature." Ph.D. diss., University of California-Berkeley, 1978.

Petty, Richard J. "Asherah: Goddess of Israel." Ph.D. diss., Marquette University, 1985.

Pfeiffer, Robert H. *Introduction to the Old Testament.* New York: Harper & Brothers, 1946.

Phillips, Anthony. "Deuteronomy." In *The Cambridge Commentary in the New English Bible*, edited by P. R. Ackroyd, A. R. C. Leaney, and J. W. Packer. Cambridge: Cambridge University Press, 1973.

Polzin, Robert. *Moses and the Deuteronomist: A Literary Study of the Deuteronomistic History. Part One—Deuteronomy, Joshua, Judges.* New York: Seabury Press, 1980.

————. "Reporting Speech in the Book of Deuteronomy: Toward a Compositional Analysis of the Deuteronomic History." In *Traditions in Transformation: Turning Points in Biblical Faith*, edited by Baruch Halpern and Jon D. Levenson, 193–211. Winona Lake, Ind.: Eisenbrauns, 1981.

————. *Samuel and the Deuteronomist: A Literary Study of the Deuteronomic History. Part Two—I Samuel.* San Francisco: Harper & Row, 1989.

Pope, Marvin H. "El in the Ugaritic Texts." In Vol. 2 of *Supplements to Vetus Testamentum*, edited by G. W. Anderson, P. A. H. De Boer, Millar Burrows, Henri Cazelles, E. Hammershaimb, and Martin Noth. Leiden: E. J. Brill, 1955.

————. "Mot." In Vol. 5 of *The Interpreter's Dictionary of the Bible*, edited by George A. Buttrick, Thomas Samuel Kepler, John Knox, Herbert Gordon May, Samuel Terrein, and Emory Stevens Bucker, 607–8. Nashville: Abingdon Press, 1982.

————. "Number, Numbering, Numbers." In Vol. 3 of *The Interpreter's Dictionary of the Bible*, edited by George A. Buttrick, Thomas Samuel Kepler, John Knox, Herbert Gordon May, Samuel Terrein, and Emory Stevens Bucker. Nashville: Abingdon Press, 1982.

_____. "Seven, Seventh, Seventy." In Vol. 4 of *The Interpreter's Dictionary of the Bible*, edited by George A. Buttrick, Thomas Samuel Kepler, John Knox, Herbert Gordon May, Samuel Terrein, and Emory Stevens Bucker. Nashville: Abingdon Press, 1982.

_____. "The Status of El at Ugarit." *Ugarit-Forschungen* 19 (1987): 219–30.

Porter, J. R. "Old Testament Historiography." In *Tradition and Interpretation*, edited by G. W. Anderson. Oxford: Clarendon Press, 1979.

Pritchard, James B. *The Ancient Near East in Pictures Relating to the Old Testament*. Princeton, N.J.: Princeton University Press, 1954.

_____. *Archaeology and the Old Testament*. London: Princeton University Press, 1958.

_____. *Palestinian Figurines In Relation To Certain Goddesses Known Through Literature*, edited by Zellig S. Harris, American Oriental Series 24. New Haven, Conn.: American Oriental Society, 1943.

Pritchard, James B., ed. *Ancient Near Eastern Texts*. Princeton: Princeton University Press, 1950.

Propp, William Henry. "Water in the Wilderness: The Mythological Background of a Biblical Motif." Ph.D. diss., Harvard University, 1985.

Rabin, C. "Judges V,2 and the 'Ideology' of Deborah's War." *Journal of Jewish Studies* 6 (1955): 125–34.

Rainey, A. F. "A Canaanite at Ugarit." *Israel Exploration Journal* 13 (1963): 43–45.

Reymond, Philippe. "L'eau, sa vie, et sa signification dans l'Ancien Testament." In Vol. 6 of *Supplements to Vetus Testamentum,* edited by G. W. Anderson, P. A. H. De Boer, Millar Burrows, Henri Cazelles, E. Hammershaimb, and Martin Noth. Leiden: E. J. Brill, 1958.

Roberts, J. J. M. "The Ancient Near Eastern Environment." In *The Hebrew Bible and Its Modern Interpreters,* edited by Douglas A. Knight and Gene M. Tucker. Philadelphia: Scholars Press Club, 1985.

Robertson, David A. *Linguistic Evidence In Dating Early Hebrew Poetry.* Missoula, Mont.: SBL, for the University of Montana, 1972.

Rowley, H. H. "Elijah on Mount Carmel." *Bulletin of the John Rylands Library* 43 (1960): 190–219.

————. "Israel, History of (Israelites)." In Vol. 2 of *The Interpreter's Dictionary of the Bible,* edited by George A. Buttrick, Thomas Samuel Kepler, John Knox, Herbert Gordon May, Samuel Terrein, and Emory Stevens Bucker. Nashville: Abingdon Press, 1982.

————. *Men of God.* London: Nelson, 1963.

Sarna, Nahum M. *Exploring Exodus: The Heritage of Biblical Israel.* New York: Schocken Books, 1986.

Save-Soderberg, T. "The Hyksos Rule Egypt." *Journal of Egyptian Archaeology* 37 (December 1951): 53–71.

Sawyer, John F. A. "From Heaven Fought The Stars, (Judges V 20)." *Vetus Testamentum* 31 (1981): 87–89.

Saydon, Paul P. "The Crossing of the Jordan, Josue 3;4." *The Catholic Biblical Quarterly* 12 (1950): 194–207.

Schaeffer, Claude F. A. *The Cuneiform Texts of Ras Shamra-Ugarit.* Published for the British Academy by Humphrey Milford Publishers. London: Oxford University Press, 1939.

Scholbies, Hans Martin. "Der akkadische Wettergott in Mesopotamien." Ph.D. diss., Philosophische Fakultät der Friedrich-Wilhelm-Universität zu Berlin, 1925.

Scott, R. B. Y. "Palestine, Climate of." In Vol. 3 of *The Interpreter's Dictionary of the Bible*, edited by George A. Buttrick, Thomas Samuel Kepler, John Knox, Herbert Gordon May, Samuel Terrein, and Emory Stevens Bucker. Nashville: Abingdon Press, 1982.

Shechter, Jack. "The Theology of the Land of Deuteronomy." Ph.D. diss., University of Michigan, 1985.

Shires, Henry H., and Pierson Parker. "The Book of Deuteronomy." In Vol. 2 of *The Interpreter's Bible*, edited by George A. Buttrick, Walter Russell Bowie, Paul Scherer, John Knox, Samuel Terrien, and Nolan B. Harmon. Nashville: Abingdon Press, 1953.

Smith, George Adam. *The Historical Geography of the Holy Land.* 25th ed. London: Hodder and Stoughton, 1931.

Smith, Henry Preserved. *A Critical and Exegetical Commentary on the Books of Samuel.* Vol. 8 of *The International Critical Commentary*, edited by S. R. Driver, Alfred Plummer, and C. A. Briggs. New York: Charles Scribner's Sons, 1899.

Smith, Mark S. "Baal's Cosmic Secret." *Ugarit-Forschungen* 16 (1984): 295–98.

———. "Interpreting the Baal Cycle." *Ugarit-Forschungen* 18 (1986): 313–39.

Snaith, Norman N. "The First and Second Books of Kings." In Vol. 3 of *The Interpreter's Dictionary of the Bible*, edited by George A. Buttrick, Thomas Samuel Kepler, John Knox, Herbert Gordon

May, Samuel Terrein, and Emory Stevens Bucker. Nashville: Abingdon Press, 1982.

Soggin, J. Alberto. *Introducion to the Old Testament.* Translated by J. Bowden. London: SCM Press, 1976.

_____. *Introduction to the Old Testament: From Its Origin to the Closing of the Alexandrian Canon.* 3d ed. Louisville, Ky.: Westminster/John Knox Press, 1989.

_____. *Judges: A Commentary.* 2d ed. Translated by John Bowden. London: SCM Press. 1987.

Stadelmann, Rainer. "Syrisch-Palastinensische Gotteiten in Agypten." In Funfter Band, *Probleme Der Agyptologie,* Herausgeben von Wolfgang Helck. Leiden: E. J. Brill, 1967.

Sutcliffe, E. F. "The Clouds as Water-Carriers in Hebrew Thought." *Vetus Testamentum* 3 (1953): 99–107.

Szikszai, Stephen. "Elijah the Prophet." In Vol. 2 of *The Interpreter's Dictionary of the Bible,* edited by George A. Buttrick, Thomas Samuel Kepler, John Knox, Herbert Gordon May, Samuel Terrein, and Emory Stevens Bucker. Nashville: Abingdon Press, 1982.

Talmon, Shernaryahu. "The 'Desert Motif' in the Bible and in Qumran Literature." In *Biblical Motifs: Origins and Transformations,* edited by Alexander Altmann. Cambridge: Harvard University Press, 1966.

The Interpreter's Bible: The Holy Scriptures in the King James and Standard Versions with General Articles and Introduction, Exegesis, Exposition for Each Book of the Bible, in Twelve Volumes. Vols. 2 and 3 edited by George A. Buttrick, Walter Russell Bowie, Paul Scherer, John Knox, Samuel Terrein, and Nolan B. Harmon. New York: Abingdon Press, 1954.

Thompson, Thomas L. *The Historicity of the Patriarchal Narratives: The Quest for the Historical Abraham*. New York: Walter de Gruyter, 1974.

Tolkowsky, S. "Gideon's Fleece." *Journal of the Palestine Oriental Society* 3 (1923): 197–99.

Toombs, Lawrence E. "Baal, Lord of the Earth: The Ugaritic Epic." In *The Word of the Lord Will Go Forth: Essays in Honor of D. N. Freedman*, edited by Carol L. Meyers and Michael O'Connor, 613–23. Winona Lake, Ind.: Eisenbrauns, 1983.

Torezyner, H. *The Lachish Letters: Lachis I*. Oxford: Oxford University Press, 1938.

Trigger, B. G., B. J. Kemp, D. O'Connor, and A. B. Lloyd. *Ancient Egypt: A Social History*. New York: Cambridge University Press, 1983.

Tromp, Nicholas J. "Water and Fire on Mount Carmel: A Conciliatory Suggestion." *Biblica* 56 (1975): 480–502.

Tsumura, David Toshio. *The Earth and the Waters in Genesis 1 and 2: A Linguistic Investigation*. Sheffield: JSOT Press, 1989.

Unterman, Jeremiah. "Gideon." In *Harper's Bible Dictionary*, edited by Paul J. Achtemeier, Roger S. Borass, Michael Fishbane, Pheme Perkins, and William O. Walker, Jr. San Francisco: Harper & Row, 1985.

Van Rooy, H. F. "The Relationship Between Anat and Baal in the Ugaritic Texts." *Journal of Northwest Semitic Languages* 7 (1979): 85–95.

Van Seters, John. *The Hyksos: A New Investigation*. New Haven, Conn.: Yale University Press, 1966.

————. *In Search of History: Historiography in the Ancient World and the Origins of Biblical History*. New Haven, Conn.: Yale University Press, 1983.

van Zijl, Peter J. "Baal: A Study of Texts in Connexion with Baal in the Uaritic Epics." In *Alter Orient und Altes Testament: Veröentlichugen zur Kultur und Geschichte des Alten Orients und des Alten Testaments*, edited by Kurt Bergerhof, Manfried Dietrich, and Oswald Loretz. Neukirchen-Vluyn: Verlag Butzon & Bercker Kevelaer, 1972.

Vine, Kenneth Lawrence. "The Establishment of Baal at Ugarit." Ph.D. diss, University of Michigan, 1965.

von Rad, Gerhard. "The Deuteronomistic Theology of History in the Book of Kings." In *Studies in Deuteronomy*, no. 9 of Studies in Biblical Theology Series, translated by David Stalker. London: SCM Press, 1953.

————. "Deuteronomy." In Vol. 1 of *The Interpreter's Dictionary of the Bible*, edited by George A. Buttrick, Thomas Samuel Kepler, John Knox, Herbert Gordon May, Samuel Terrein, and Emory Stevens Bucker. Nashville: Abingdon Press, 1982.

————. "Deuteronomy: A Commentary." In *The Old Testament Library*, edited by G. E. Wright, John Bright, James Barr, and Peter Ackroyd, translated by Dorothea Barton. Philadelphia: Westminster Press, 1966.

————. *Old Testament Theology, Vol. II: The Theology of Israel's Prophetic Traditions*. Translated by D. M. G. Stalker. New York: Harper & Row, 1965.

————. *The Problem of the Texateuch and Other Essays*. Translated by Trueman Dicken. New York: McGraw-Hill, 1966.

————. *Studies in Deuteronomy*. Chicago: Henry Regnery Co., 1953.

von Waldow, Hans Eberhard. "Israel and Her Land: Some Theological Consideration." In *A Light unto My Path: Old Testament Studies in Honor of Jacob M. Myers*, edited by Howard N. Bream, Ralph D. Heim, and Carey A, Moore. Philadelphia: Temple University Press, 1974.

Wakeman, Mary K. *God's Battle with the Monster: A Study in Biblical Imagery*. Leiden: E. J. Brill, 1973.

Watson, Paul L. "The Death of 'Death' in the Ugaritic Texts." *Journal of the American Oriental Society* 92 (January-March 1972): 60–64.

————. "Mot, The God of Death at Ugarit and in the Old Testament." Ph.D. diss., Yale University, 1970.

Webb, Barry G. *The Book of Judges*. Sheffield: Academic Press, 1987.

Weimar, Peter. "Die Jahwekriegserzählungen in Exodus 14, Joshua 10, Richter 4 und I Samuel 7." *Biblica* 57 (1976): 38–73, fasc. 1.

Weinfeld, Moshe. *Deuteronomy and the Deuteronomic School*. Oxford: Clarendon Press, 1972.

————. "Deuteronomy—The Present State of Inquiry." *Journal of Biblical Literature* 86 (1967): 249–62.

————. "Divine Intervention in War in Ancient Israel and in the Ancient Near East." In *History, Historiography and Interpretation: Studies in Bibical and Cuneiform Languages*, edited by H. Tadmor and M. Weinfeld, 121–47. Leiden: E. J. Brill, 1983.

————. "'Rider of the Clouds' and 'Gatherer of the Clouds.'" *Journal of the Ancient Near Eastern Society of Columbia University* 5 (1973): 421–26.

Wellhausen, Julius. *Prolegomena to the History of Ancient Israel*. Cleveland: The World Publishing Co., Meridian Book, 1961.

Whiston, William, trans. *Josephus Complete Works*. Grand Rapids, Mich.: Kregel Publications, 1978.

Whitaker, Richard E. *A Concordance of the Ugaritic Literature*. Cambridge: Harvard University Press, 1972.

Whitley, C. F. "The Sources of the Gideon Stories." *Vetus Testamentum* 7 (1957): 157–64.

Wijngaards, J. N. S. *The Dramatization of Salvific History in the Deuteronomic Schools*. Leiden: E. J. Brill, 1969.

Wiseman, D. J. "The Vassal-Treaties of Esarhaddon." *Iraq* 20 (1958): 1–99.

Wolff, Hans Walter. "The Kerygma of the Deuteronomic Historical Work." Translated by Frederick Prussner. In Walter Brueggeman and Hans Walter Wolff, *The Vitality of Old Testament Traditions*, 2d ed. Atlanta: John Knox Press, 1982.

Worden, T. "The Literary Influence of the Ugaritic Fertility Myth on the Old Testament." *Vetus Testamentum* 3 (1953): 273–97.

Wright, G. Ernest. "The Old Testament Against Its Environment." In number 2 of *Studies in Biblical Theology*. London: SCM Press, 1950.

Wyatt, N. "The Source of the Ugaritic Myth of the Conflict of Ba'al and Yam." *Ugarit-Forschungen* 20 (1988): 375–85.

Yadin, Yigael. "The 'House of Ba'al' of Ahab and Jezebel in Samaria, and that of Athalia in Judah." In *Archaeology in the Levant: Essays for Kathleen Kenyon*, edited by Roger Moorey and Peter Parr, 127–35. Warminster, England: Aris and Phillips, 1978.

Yeivin, S. "Ya'qob'el." *The Journal of Egyptian Archaeology* 45 (1959): 16–18.

Zandee, J. "Seth als Sturmgott." *Zeitschrift für ägyptische sprache und Ältertumskunde* 90 (1963): 144–56.

Zevit, Ziony. "Deuteronomic Historiography in I Kings 12–17 and the Reinvestiture of the Israelian Cult." *Journal of the Study of the Old Testament* 32 (1985): 57–73.

INDEX

Z

DATE DUE